CliffsNotes

D0199026

Twain's

Adventures of Huckleberry Finn

By Robert Bruce, Ph.D.

IN THIS BOOK

- Learn about the Life and Background of the Author
- Preview an Introduction to the Novel
- Study a graphical Character Map
- Explore themes and literary devices in the Critical Commentaries
- Examine in-depth Character Analyses
- Reinforce what you learn with CliffsNotes Review
- Find additional information to further your study in CliffsNotes Resource Center and online at www.cliffsnotes.com

IDG Books Worldwide, Inc.
An International Data Group Company
Foster City, CA • Chicago, IL • Indianapolis, IN • New York, NY

About the Author

Robert Bruce currently teaches American Humor and is Director of the Texas Annual Fund at the University of Texas at Austin. He graduated with a Ph.D. in English from Texas A&M University with a specialization in Mark Twain and American Humor.

Publisher's Acknowledgments

Editorial

Project Editor: Tracy Barr
Acquisitions Editor: Greg Tubach
Editorial Administrator: Michelle Hacker
Glossary Editors: The editors and staff of Webster's New World Dictionaries

Production

Indexer: York Production Services, Inc.
Proofreader: York Production Services, Inc.
IDG Books Indianapolis Production Department

CliffsNotes™ Twain's *Adventures of Huckleberry Finn*
Published by
IDG Books Worldwide, Inc.
An International Data Group Company
919 E. Hillsdale Blvd.
Suite 400
Foster City, CA 94404

www.idgbooks.com (IDG Books Worldwide Web site)

www.cliffsnotes.com (CliffsNotes Web site)

ISBN: 0-7645-8604-1

Printed in the United States of America

10 9 8 7 6 5 4 3 2 1

1O/ST/QV/QQ/IN

Distributed in the United States by IDG Books Worldwide, Inc.

Library of Congress Cataloging-in-Publication Data
Bruce, Robert, 1968-
    CliffsNotes Twain's Adventures of Huckleberry Finn / by Robert Bruce.
      p. cm.
    ISBN 0-7645-8604-1 (alk. paper)
    1. Twain, Mark, 1835-1910. Adventures of Huckleberry Finn--Examinations--Study guides.
I. Title: Twain's Adventures of Huckleberry Finn.
II. Title.

PS1305 .B78 2000
813'.4--dc21   00-038849
                                                            CIP

Distributed by CDG Books Canada Inc. for Canada; by Transworld Publishers Limited in the United Kingdom; by IDG Norge Books for Norway; by IDG Sweden Books for Sweden; by IDG Books Australia Publishing Corporation Pty. Ltd. for Australia and New Zealand; by TransQuest Publishers Pte Ltd. for Singapore, Malaysia, Thailand, Indonesia, and Hong Kong; by Gotop Information Inc. for Taiwan; by ICG Muse, Inc. for Japan; by Intersoft for South Africa; by Eyrolles for France; by International Thomson Publishing for Germany, Austria and Switzerland; by Distribuidora Cuspide for Argentina; by LR International for Brazil; by Galileo Libros for Chile; by Ediciones ZETA S.C.R. Ltda. for Peru; by WS Computer Publishing Corporation, Inc., for the Philippines; by Contemporanea de Ediciones for Venezuela; by Express Computer Distributors for the Caribbean and West Indies; by Micronesia Media Distributor, Inc. for Micronesia; by Chips Computadoras S.A. de C.V. for Mexico; by Editorial Norma de Panama S.A. for Panama; by American Bookshops for Finland.

For general information on IDG Books Worldwide's books in the U.S., please call our Consumer Customer Service department at **800-762-2974.** For reseller information, including discounts and premium sales, please call our Reseller Customer Service department at **800-434-3422.**

For information on where to purchase IDG Books Worldwide's books outside the U.S., please contact our International Sales department at **317-596-5530** or fax **317-572-4002.**

For consumer information on foreign language translations, please contact our Customer Service department at **1-800-434-3422,** fax 317-572-4002, or e-mail rights@idgbooks.com.

For information on licensing foreign or domestic rights, please phone **+1-650-653-7098.**

For sales inquiries and special prices for bulk quantities, please contact our Order Services department at **800-434-3422** or write to the address above.

For information on using IDG Books Worldwide's books in the classroom or for ordering examination copies, please contact our Educational Sales department at **800-434-2086** or fax **317-572-4005.**

For press review copies, author interviews, or other publicity information, please contact our Public Relations department at **650-653-7000** or fax **650-653-7500.**

For authorization to photocopy items for corporate, personal, or educational use, please contact Copyright Clearance Center, 222 Rosewood Drive, Danvers, MA 01923, or fax **978-750-4470.**

Table of Contents

How to Use This Book

CliffsNotes on Mark Twain's *Adventures of Huckleberry Finn* supplements the original work, giving you background information about the author, an introduction to the novel, a graphical character map, critical commentaries, expanded glossaries, and a comprehensive index. CliffsNotes Review tests your comprehension of the original text and reinforces learning with questions and answers, practice projects, and more. For further information on Mark Twain and *Adventures of Huckleberry Finn,* check out the CliffsNotes Resource Center.

CliffsNotes provides the following icons to highlight essential elements of particular interest:

Reveals the underlying themes in the work.

Helps you to more easily relate to or discover the depth of a character.

Uncovers elements such as setting, atmosphere, mystery, passion, violence, irony, symbolism, tragedy, foreshadowing, and satire.

Enables you to appreciate the nuances of words and phrases.

Don't Miss Our Web Site

Discover classic literature as well as modern-day treasures by visiting the CliffsNotes Web site at www.cliffsnotes.com. You can obtain a quick download of a CliffsNotes title, purchase a title in print form, browse our catalog, or view online samples.

You'll also find interactive tools that are fun and informative, links to interesting Web sites, tips, articles, and additional resources to help you, not only for literature, but for test prep, finance, careers, computers, and the Internet too. See you at www.cliffsnotes.com!

LIFE AND BACKGROUND OF THE AUTHOR

Personal Background

Perhaps it was a sign of the infant's rise to literary fame. As Halley's comet reached its perihelion—its closest point to the sun—Samuel Langhorne Clemens was born in the sleepy, little town of Florida, Missouri, on November 30, 1835. No one realized, of course, that the fifth child of John and Jane Clemens would eventually become more famous than the celebrated comet and recognized as one of the most original and important authors in American and world literature. His legacy extends to that of America's greatest humorist, and his abundance of works reflects his early years along the country's great river.

Sam's father, John Marshall Clemens, a highly intelligent man, was a mildly successful lawyer, a justice of the peace, and a stern disciplinarian of his children. Sam's mother, Jane, a Southern belle in her youth, had a natural sense of humor and was greatly affectionate, especially to animals and people down on their luck. The combination of parental personalities would later be found in several of Mark Twain's characters, and Huckleberry Finn's concern for the less fortunate is reminiscent of Jane Clemen's kindness and compassion.

When Sam reached the age of four, the family moved to Hannibal, Missouri, a small town of about a thousand people. Situated on the West bank of the Mississippi River, roughly eighty miles north of St. Louis, Hannibal was dusty, quiet, and in walking distance of large forests. The surrounding land and waterways provided young Sam countless images for his future writings. The Mississippi River shoreline was constantly occupied with rafts, skiffs, and large steamboats moving up and down the main artery between the North and the South. The tanyard, where Pap Finn would later sleep among the hogs, was found nearby, and downstream was a small cave where Indian Joe would later trap Tom and Becky in *The Adventures of Tom Sawyer.* Hannibal would eventually become "St. Petersburg" in *Tom Sawyer* and the same town was used for the initial setting in *Huck Finn.*

With its rustic landscape, bustling river traffic, and scores of eager pioneers passing through on their way to fortune in the West, Hannibal introduced Sam to an America that was quickly moving out of the frontier age. More important, the town introduced the young boy to two substantial aspects of American life: the concept of slavery and the reality of death. Although Missouri was a slave state, Hannibal's northern position resulted in a part slave/part free community. At that time, Sam did not trouble himself with the distinction. His recollections of childhood included his attitude toward slavery, and he later acknowledged that he was unaware of its inhumanity: "I had no aversion to slavery. I was not aware that there was anything wrong about it."

Early Career

The death of the father in 1847 placed the Clemens family in financial difficulty, and Sam had to forego the schooling he had begun and become an apprentice printer to the publisher of the local *Missouri Courier*. Shortly thereafter, Sam left to work as an apprentice for his brother, Orion. The brothers returned to Hannibal after two years, and Orion took control as proprietor of the *Journal*. In addition to his apprentice duties, Sam contributed small literary pieces to the *Journal*, a humble beginning to his future writing career. The success of the brothers was short-lived, however, and after Orion left Hannibal, Sam found work in St. Louis, then New York, and Philadelphia. For a brief period of time, he joined his brother Orion in Keokuk, Iowa, where he again worked as a printer.

In 1856, hoping to find the success that had eluded his father and Orion, Sam conceived a wild scheme of making a fortune in South America. The drive to become rich quickly through promising deals would follow Sam throughout his life. On a riverboat to New Orleans, however, Sam met a riverboat pilot who promised to teach him the trade for five hundred dollars. Because of his fascination with the river and the grand boats that traveled it, Sam seized the opportunity to become a pilot of the muddy waters. In 1857, he became a cub pilot on the *Paul Jones* steamboat, eventually receiving his pilot's license in 1859. After completing his training, he was a riverboat pilot for four years, during which time he became familiar with the towns along the Mississippi River and their various inhabitants.

When the American Civil War broke out in April of 1861, the Mississippi River was effectively closed by both Union and Confederate forces, and Sam was forced to abandon his pilot career. Sam, whose allegiance tended to be Southern due to his heritage, joined the Confederate militia, but after three short weeks, he deserted and headed West. In his *Autobiography*, Twain remarked that "I resigned after two weeks service in the field, explaining that I was 'incapacitated by fatigue' through persistent retreating." Orion convinced him to join an expedition to the Nevada Territory, a trip that became the subject matter of a later work, *Roughing It* (1872).

Writing Career

While in the Nevada Territory, Sam resumed writing humorous sketches and travel letters and began using the pseudonym, Mark Twain, a term for water that is only two fathoms—twelve feet—deep. Twain continued to sign his more serious pieces as "S. L. Clemens," but the farces, hoaxes, and satires that were to make him famous were now authored by "Mark Twain." With the realization that he had an audience for his brand of bawdy humor, Twain began to travel extensively and write humorous travel letters for the *San Francisco Alta California*. The *Alta California* sponsored his steamship journey from New York to the Mediterranean, and the resulting travel letters increased his audience and admirers; Twain's literary rise was under way.

Between 1864 and 1870, Twain contributed articles and travel letters to various newspapers and published *Innocents Abroad* (1869). After a long courtship, he married Olivia Langdon, daughter of Jervis Langdon, in 1870. Olivia proved to be a tempering influence on the often-moody Twain, and her family's abolitionist views on slavery influenced Twain and his writings. As with Olivia's father, Jervis, Twain eventually became friends with Frederick Douglass and supported the antislavery movement.

Because of the acclaim of *Innocents Abroad*, Twain gave up his career as a journalist-reporter and began concentrating on short stories and books. Using the method of parlaying his short story success into collections, Twain's fame as a writer was immediate, and *Innocents Abroad* became a bestseller. The satire Twain used to expose the so-called sophistication of the Old World, in contrast to the old-fashioned American common sense, is similar to that found some ten years later in *A Tramp Abroad* (1880), *The Prince and the Pauper* (1881), and *A Connecticut Yankee in King Arthur's Court* (1889), when Hank Morgan confronts nobility and knighthood.

But it was the Mississippi River and the values of the people living along its shores that have made Twain one of America's best and favorite storytellers. The humor that he found among the small one-horse towns, along with the culture of the Mississippi, has continued to fascinate readers and to embody an almost mythic sense of what it meant to be a young American in the latter part of the nineteenth century.

In 1876, Twain captured these elements in *The Adventures of Tom Sawyer*. Despite its contemporary reception, *Tom Sawyer's* publication was overshadowed by the deaths of George Custer and his calvary at

Little Big Horn. But the book's popularity would grow throughout Twain's lifetime, and by the time of his death, it was his best-selling novel. Twain's most controversial work, however, was to come nine years later. In 1885, the *Adventures of Huckleberry Finn* was published among much publicity and fanfare. *Huck Finn* ensured Twain's place among the literary giants, and the work would prove to be Twain's most studied and critically acclaimed novel.

Later Years

After Twain turned fifty, his fortunes reversed themselves. His health began to fail, and in 1894, he was forced to declare bankruptcy due to his investment in a failed automatic typesetter, a publishing company that drained more of his money than it earned him. His failures with moneymaking ventures extended to his family, and he suffered through the illnesses and deaths of those whom he loved. His wife, Olivia, struggled with her health and soon became a semi-invalid; one of his daughters developed epilepsy; and his oldest daughter died of meningitis. Twain's comment that "the secret source of Humor itself is not joy but sorrow" became painfully realized, and by the end of the nineteenth century, Twain's writings reflected his dark view of life.

Overall, the 1890s were Twain's blackest decade. Twain and his family lived throughout Europe in hopes that the weather would improve the health of all the family members, but they sorely missed their home in Hartford, Connecticut, and the Langdon house at Quarry Farm in Elmira, New York. In 1894, Twain published *Pudd'nhead Wilson*, in which he confronted the slave-holding South and the question of nature versus nurture. Following a lecture trip around the world to raise money to repay his many creditors, he brought out a series of mostly unremarkable books, including *Personal Recollections of Joan of Arc*, *Tom Sawyer Abroad*, and *Tom Sawyer, Detective*, all published in 1896.

In 1900, Twain's short story "The Man That Corrupted Hadleyburg" was printed and proved to be one of his bleakest works. In it, Twain argued that human beings have no choice in what they do, no matter how much they think they are free to choose; rather, decisions are based selfishly on what will best help the individual. Twain's only darker view of humanity, published posthumously, was the fragmented *The Mysterious Stranger*, in which he condemned the universe and mocked the pitiful relations to one another and God.

On April 19, 1910, some 75 years after its last appearance, Halley's comet again reached its perihelion. Two days later, American's greatest humorist died at sunset at Stormfield, Twain's home near Redding, Connecticut. Olivia had died almost six years earlier, and Twain—"worn out in body and spirit," according to one critic—greatly missed his wife's company.

His Body of Work

The body of work that Twain left behind is immense and varied—poetry, sketches, journalistic pieces, political essays, novels, and short stories—all a testament to the diverse talent and energy that used the folklore of frontier America to create authentic masterpieces of enduring value. Many of his novels, especially those written earlier in his career, continue to be reprinted, and none rivals the overwhelming success of *Adventures of Huckleberry Finn*, which continues to be one of the most read, discussed, and taught novels in American culture. In one of Twain's letters to William Dean Howells, Twain captured his own view of his life and his works: "Ah, well, I am a great & sublime fool. But then I am God's fool, & all His works must be contemplated with respect."

Following is a publication history of Twain's novels and important works:

1865	"Jim Smiley and His Jumping Frog"
1867	*The Celebrated Jumping Frog of Calaveras County, and Other Sketches with the Burlesque Autobiography and First Romance*
1868	"The Man Who Put up at Gadsby's"
	"The Facts Concerning the Recent Resignation"
1869	*The Innocents Abroad, or The new Pilgrims' Progress; Being some Account of the Steamship Quaker City's Pleasure Excursion to Europe*
	"A Day at Niagra"
1870	"A Medieval Romance"
	"A Curious Dream"
	"A Ghost Story"

1871   *Mark Twain's (Burlesque) Autobiography*

         Roughing It

1873   *The Gilded Age*

1874   *The Choice Humorous Works of Mark Twain*

1875   "Old Times on the Mississippi" (serial)

         Sketches, New and Old

         "The Curious Republic of Gondour"

1876   *The Adventures of Tom Sawyer*

         begins *Adventures of Huckleberry Finn*

1877   *A True Story and the Recent Carnival of Crime*

1878   *Punch, Brothers Punch! and Other Sketches*

1880   *A Tramp Abroad*

1881   *The Prince and the Pauper*

1882   *The Stolen White Elephant*

1883   *Life on the Mississippi* (Chapter 3, the "Raft Chapter" was originally in *Adventures of Huckleberry Finn*. The character, Jim, is introduced in this chapter.)

         finishes *Adventures of Huckleberry Finn*

1884   **Extracts of *Adventures of Huckleberry* Finn are published in *Century Magazine***

         ***Adventures of Huckleberry Finn (Tom Sawyer's Comrade)* (London, Canada)**

1885   ***Adventures of Huckleberry Finn (Tom Sawyer's Comrade)* (New York)**

1888   *Mark Twain's Library of Humor*

1889   *A Connecticut Yankee in King Arthur's Court*

1892   *Merry Tales*

         The American Claimant

1893	*The 1,000,000 Bank-Note and Other Stories*
1894	*Tom Sawyer Abroad*
	Pudd'nhead Wilson
1895	"How to Tell a Story"
1896	*Personal Recollections of Joan of Arc*
	Tom Sawyer Abroad/Tom Sawyer, Detective and Other Stories
1897	*How to Tell a Story and Other Essays*
	Following the Equator
	"The Chronicle of Young Satan"
	"The Mysterious Stranger"
1900	*The Man That Corrupted Hadleyburg and Other Essays*
	English as She is Taught
1902	*A Double-Barrelled Detective Story*
1903	*My Debut as a Literary Person with Others Essays and Stories*
1904	*A Dog's Tale*
1905	*King Leopold's Soliloquy*
1906	*The $30,000 Bequest and Other Stories*
	What is Man?
1907	*Christian Science*
	A Horse's Tale
1909	*Is Shakespeare Dead*
	Extract from Captain Stormfield's Visit to Heaven
1910	"The Turning Point in My Life"

INTRODUCTION TO THE NOVEL

Introduction

In 1876, the same year as the publication of *The Adventures of Tom Sawyer,* Mark Twain began work on another boy's tale of adventure along the Mississippi. After deciding that Tom was unfit to narrate the book, Twain chose Tom's counterpart, the disreputable Huckleberry Finn. Huck was already well known to an American audience thirsting for more of Twain's brand of humor, and Twain hoped to capitalize on his recent literary successes. Despite the end of the Civil War in 1865, it was a tumultuous time for America. Southern Reconstruction had fallen into disarray, and a new racism of segregation and condoned inequality replaced the slavery that had been abolished with the Emancipation Proclamation.

Twain's original intention, as he stated to William Dean Howells, was to take "a boy of twelve and run him on through life (in the first person)." In the aftermath of the war and the failure of Reconstruction, however, the work quickly bogged down as the book began to address the issue of freedom and slavery; it was not a path that Twain was eager to take. After writing the first few chapters, Twain's inspiration for the tale began to fade, and he set aside the work to pursue other projects such as *A Tramp Abroad* (1880) and *The Prince and the Pauper* (1881).

In 1882, Twain again took up the manuscript and began developing the story of the young, white boy named Huck and the enslaved, black man named Jim. He worked sporadically over the next two years and finished the manuscript in July of 1883. Two years later, in February of 1885, Huck Finn reintroduced himself to American readers: "You don't know about me without you have read a book by the name of *The Adventures of Tom Sawyer*; but that ain't no matter."

Huck's journey down the Mississippi River has been called an odyssey by some and a pilgrimage by others. Indeed, characteristics of each abound. Like Homer's *Odyssey,* the novel is episodic—that is, it is composed of a series of episodes—and in many ways Huck's adventure is a pilgrimage (a journey of exalted purpose or moral). Some consider the novel to be of the picaresque genre, which originated in Spain and depicts in realistic detail the adventures of a roguish hero, often with satiric or humorous effects. Others contend that Huck does not fit the role of rogue and that, therefore, the novel does not qualify as picaresque.

Twain did not consider the novel his best work, and he was completely unprepared for the reception that would follow. In a caustic review immediately following *Huck Finn's* publication, *Life* magazine condemned the book that contained graphic instances of nudity and death. The Concord Public Library followed by declaring the book held little humor and regarded it as the "veriest trash." And popular author Louisa May Alcott echoed the sentiments by saying that perhaps Twain should stop writing for American boys and girls altogether if this was the only work he could offer.

Although several initial reviews were negative, *Adventures of Huckleberry Finn* was also quickly commended as an American classic for its expression of the American imagination. The ability to adapt to any situation, the tranquility and promise of the country's great river, and the colorful and varied characters that inhabited the vanishing frontier are all represented within its pages. These elements prompted one of the most famous observations about *Huck Finn* in 1935, when Ernest Hemingway remarked that "all modern American literature comes from one book by Mark Twain called *Huckleberry Finn* . . .. It's the best book we've had. All American writing comes from that. There was nothing before. There has been nothing as good since." The novel is, indeed, a masterful display of hoaxes, frauds, and pranks, all elements of American humor that Twain had explored in his own readings and previous writings.

No author before Twain had been able to blend the American condition in such a fascinating and engaging manner. It is not surprising then, that 115 years later, close to 1,000 different editions of *Huck Finn* have been published since the novel first appeared as *Adventures of Huckleberry Finn (Tom Sawyer's Comrade)*. The translations number more than 100, and the amount of scholarly articles and books continue to dominate the study of American literature. Critical interpretations run the gamut from expansive social commentary of post-Reconstruction in the South, to linguistic interpretations of the African-American voice, to exploration of dark humor and the mythical trickster character. The book has continued to invite exegesis and ignite controversy, and its position as an American classic appears to be ensured.

Simply put, the book continues to thrive because of its original narrative style, its realistic subject matter, and its depiction of loyalty and sacrifice, regardless of the consequences. Unlike former southwestern humor characters, such as George Washington Harris' Sut Lovingood and Johnson J. Hooper's Simon Suggs, Huck does not rely upon an authoritative, gentleman narrator to introduce the story or help explain its significance. There is no doubt that Twain drew heavily upon his literary predecessors for inspiration, but Huck's story is his own. He tells it from his own boyish point of view, free from any affectation, underlying motive, or purpose. In doing so, Twain created a completely original American voice. As Twain scholar Hamlin Hill noted in his introduction to the centennial facsimile edition: "No major writer before Mark Twain had dared to liberate, without explanation or apology, the common character to tell his own story in his own language, and so to dramatize a realistic version of the average American."

Twain did more, however, than depict a realistic version of an average American boy, he also presented the squalid and cruel environment of the South in a brutal and raw manner, including its use of the horrid and offensive term, "niggers." The unabashed narrative approach to racism and the American condition prompted American author Langston Hughes to comment that Twain's work "punctured some of the pretenses of the romantic Old South." By allowing Huck to tell his own story, Twain used his realistic fiction to address America's most painful "sacred cow": the contradiction of racism and segregation in a "free" and "equal" society.

It is ironic that *Huck Finn* is currently banned in several school libraries for its content and language. Twain's original fears were also of censorship, yet his concern was that the novel would be denounced because of its positive portrayal of Jim and its realistic depiction of the South. To mask his content, Twain infused satire and dark humor throughout the novel. Thus Huck's tale is filled with both moments of childish adventure and instances of biting satire.

The rhetorical coupling of childhood fantasies and death is subtle, and yet the technique of providing the dream of the perfect boyhood allows Twain to use subsequent incongruities for the purposes of social satire. Huck's literal attitude is, at the same time, puerile and mature. In the childlike guise, he views his surroundings in a sensory manner; his environment is constructed and solidified by what he sees and hears. In the adult guise, Huck displays an uncanny wisdom that goes beyond his years as he subconsciously conveys to his readers that beneath the illusion of a carefree world is a country filled with self-doubt. Because Huck is literal, he sees through the idealism and brings about a sobering and realistic revelation.

When Huck contemplates his future aboard the raft in Chapter 31, readers contemplate it with him. And when Huck firmly states, "All right, then, I'll *go* to hell," readers realize that the decision is based on emotion, as well as Huck's normal logic and pragmatism, which he never escapes. This scene in Chapter 31, for example, is reminiscent of Chapter 16, in which Huck saves Jim by deceiving the men looking for runaway slaves by intimating that there was scarlet fever on the raft. There, he felt "bad and low because I knowed very well I had done wrong . . .." He reasons, however, that he would have felt the same way if he had turned Jim in, and he concludes, " . . . what's the use of learning to do right when it's troublesome to do right and it ain't no trouble to do wrong, and the wages is just the same." In all his previous experiences, Huck retains his indifferent persona, yet, at the defining moment in Chapter 31, Twain empowers Huck with compassion, and, in doing so, establishes the philosophical possibility that both Huck and Jim can gain freedom.

At this point, readers realize that Twain has moved beyond the various pranks and farces into the realm of bitter social satire. The disquieting element in *Huck Finn* is not death but contradiction. The biting irony is that Huck constantly believes he is evil because he goes against society's tenets. Moreover, while technically Jim is free from the bonds of Southern slavery, he is also infinitely chained to societal constructions in the same manner that Huck, Tom, Aunt Polly, and the rest of Twain's world are enslaved. Twain's satirical carrot of idealism is the suggestion that one could successfully break misconceived societal norms, just like Reconstruction attempted to cure the racist ills of a divided South. In this manner, the novel explores the important historical and social underbelly of a nation coping with the existence of social incongruities such as equality and racism. The recognition of this reality in the late nineteenth century, and indeed in the new millennium, makes *Huck Finn* a novel worthy of discussion.

Ultimately, however, it is the recognition of the heroic struggles of both Huck and Jim that makes *Huck Finn* a classic work of literature. The testament to human perseverance, loyalty, and faith is embodied in the work through Huck and Jim's gestures of sacrifice. This is not to say that Huck and Jim are able to fully overcome the social obstacles that are placed before them. But the fact that the two nineteenth-century characters—an orphaned boy and a runaway slave—establish a bond that overcomes the boundaries set up by society, even for a brief, fleeting moment, is testament to the heroic truth of *Adventures of Huckleberry Finn*.

A Brief Synopsis

Consisting of 43 chapters, the novel begins with Huck Finn introducing himself as someone readers might have heard of in the past.

Readers learn that the practical Huck has become rich from his last adventure with Tom Sawyer *(The Adventures of Tom Sawyer)* and that the Widow Douglas and her sister, Miss Watson, have taken Huck into their home in order to try and teach him religion and proper manners. Instead of obeying his guardians, however, Huck sneaks out of the house at night to join Tom Sawyer's gang and pretend that they are robbers and pirates.

One day Huck discovers that his father, Pap Finn, has returned to town. Because Pap has a history of violence and drunkenness, Huck is worried about Pap's intentions, especially toward his invested money. When Pap confronts Huck and warns him to quit school and stop trying to better himself, Huck continues to attend school just to spite Pap. Huck's fears are soon realized when Pap kidnaps him and takes him across the Mississippi River to a small cabin on the Illinois shore.

Although Huck becomes somewhat comfortable with his life free from religion and school, Pap's beatings become too severe, and Huck fakes his own murder and escapes down the Mississippi. Huck lands a few miles down at Jackson's Island, and there he stumbles across Miss Watson's slave, Jim, who has run away for fear he will be sold down the river.

Huck and Jim soon learn that men are coming to search Jackson's Island, and the two fugitives escape down the river on a raft. Jim's plan is to reach the Illinois town of Cairo, and from there, he can take the Ohio River up to the free states. The plan troubles Huck and his conscience. However, Huck continues to stay with Jim as they travel, despite his belief that he is breaking all of society and religion's tenets. Huck's struggle with the concept of slavery and Jim's freedom continues throughout the novel.

Huck and Jim encounter several characters during their flight, including a band of robbers aboard a wrecked steamboat and two Southern "genteel" families who are involved in a bloody feud. The only time that Huck and Jim feel that they are truly free is when they are aboard the raft. This freedom and tranquility are shattered by the arrival of the duke and the king, who commandeer the raft and force Huck and Jim to stop at various river towns in order to perform confidence scams on the inhabitants. The scams are harmless until the duke and the king pose as English brothers and plot to steal a family's entire inheritance. Before the duke and the king can complete their plan, the real brothers arrive. In the subsequent confusion, Huck and Jim escape and are soon joined by the duke and the king.

Disappointed at their lack of income, the duke and the king betray Huck and Jim, and sell Jim back into slavery. When Huck goes to find Jim, he discovers that Jim is being held captive on Silas and Sally Phelps' farm. The Phelps think Huck is their visiting nephew, Tom Sawyer, and Huck easily falls into the role of Tom. Tom Sawyer soon arrives and, after Huck explains Jim's captivity, Tom takes on the guise of his own brother, Sid. After dismissing Huck's practical method of escape, Tom suggests they concoct an elaborate plan to free Jim. Tom's plan is haphazardly based on several of the prison and adventure novels he has read, and the simple act of freeing Jim becomes a complicated farce with rope ladders, snakes, and mysterious messages.

When the escape finally takes place, a pursuing farmer shoots Tom in the calf. Because Jim will not leave the injured Tom, Jim is again recaptured and taken back to the Phelps farm. At the farm, Tom reveals the entire scheme to Aunt Sally and Uncle Silas. Readers learn that Miss Watson has passed away and freed Jim in her will, and Tom has been aware of Jim's freedom the entire time. At the end of the novel, Jim is finally set free and Huck ponders his next adventure away from civilization.

List of Characters

Huckleberry Finn Narrator and main character of the novel.

Jim Runaway slave who joins Huck in his flight down the Mississippi.

Tom Sawyer Huck's civilized best friend who enjoys extravagant stories and schemes.

Pap Finn Huck's abusive, drunken father who plots to steal his son's reward money.

The Duke River con man who claims to be the Duke of Bridgewater and takes control of Huck and Jim's raft.

The King River con man who claims to be the disappeared heir to the French throne and takes control of Huck and Jim's raft.

Widow Douglas Town widow who tries to civilize Huck through kindness and religion.

Miss Watson Widow Douglas's sister who tries to civilize Huck through manners and religion.

Aunt Polly Tom Sawyer's aunt and guardian.

Jo Harper, Ben Rogers, and Tommy Barnes Town boys who are members of Tom Sawyer's "band of robbers."

Judge Thatcher Kindly town judge who watches over Huck's reward money.

Mrs. Loftus St. Petersburg town woman whom Huck visits disguised as a girl.

Jake Packard, Bill, and Jim Turner Gang of murderers whom Huck and Jim discover on the sinking steamboat the *Walter Scott.*

The Grangerfords Distinguished family who watches over Huck when Huck and Jim are separated. The family maintains a deadly feud with the neighboring Shepherdsons.

Buck Grangerford Youngest Grangerford boy who befriends Huck and is subsequently killed by the Shepherdsons.

Emmeline Grangerford Grangerford daughter who wrote romantic epigraphs and died at 14.

The Shepherdsons Distinguished family who feuds with the Grangerfords.

Boggs Harmless Arkansas town drunkard who is shot by Colonel Sherburn.

Colonel Sherburn The man who shoots Boggs and repels the lynch mob who comes after him.

Peter Wilks Deceased townsman. His grieving family takes in the duke, the king, and Huck as Peter Wilk's two brothers and boy servant.

William and Harvey Wilks Peter Wilks' brothers who live in England.

Mary Jane, Susan, and Joanna Peter Wilks' nieces who are tricked by the duke and the king.

Dr. Robinson and Levi Bell Two men who do not believe the duke and the king are the Wilks brothers.

Silas Phelps Tom Sawyer's uncle.

Aunt Sally Phelps Tom Sawyer's aunt.

Character Map

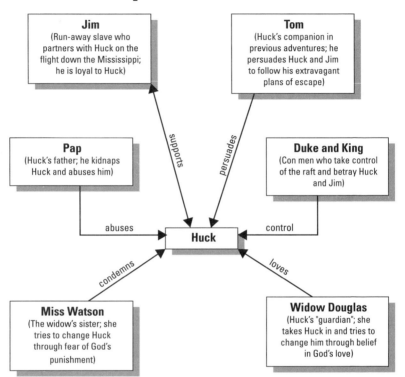

Jim
(Run-away slave who partners with Huck on the flight down the Mississippi; he is loyal to Huck)

Tom
(Huck's companion in previous adventures; he persuades Huck and Jim to follow his extravagant plans of escape)

Pap
(Huck's father; he kidnaps Huck and abuses him)

Duke and King
(Con men who take control of the raft and betray Huck and Jim)

supports

persuades

abuses

Huck

control

condemns

loves

Miss Watson
(The widow's sister; she tries to change Huck through fear of God's punishment)

Widow Douglas
(Huck's "guardian"; she takes Huck in and tries to change him through belief in God's love)

Huck Finn Geography

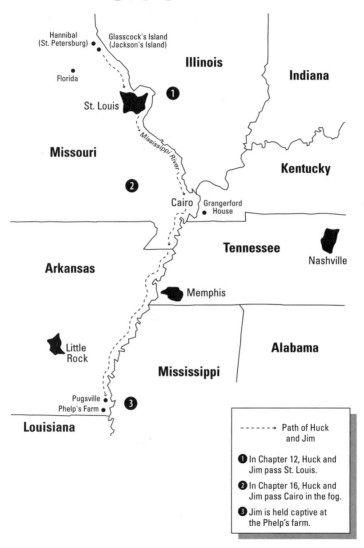

Hannibal
(St. Petersburg) •

Glasscock's Island
(Jackson's Island)

Illinois

• Florida

Indiana

St. Louis

❶

Mississippi River

Missouri

❷

Kentucky

Cairo

Grangerford
• House

Tennessee

Nashville

Arkansas

• Memphis

Little
Rock

Alabama

Mississippi

Pugsville •
Phelp's Farm •

❸

Louisiana

- - - - - → Path of Huck
and Jim

❶ In Chapter 12, Huck and
Jim pass St. Louis.

❷ In Chapter 16, Huck and
Jim pass Cairo in the fog.

❸ Jim is held captive at
the Phelp's farm.

CRITICAL COMMENTARIES

Notice; Explanatory

Summary

Twain greets readers with a "NOTICE" before he steps aside and allows Huck Finn to narrate the story. The following narrative, Twain warns, should not be analyzed for "motive" or "moral" or "plot" or punishment will follow. In the Explanatory, Twain notifies readers that characters will sound as if they live in the region in which the story takes place.

Commentary

These statements serve three purposes. First, the warning is a satiric jab at the sentimental literary style, which was in direct contrast to Twain's brand of literary realism. Second, the warning introduces the use of satire, a harsh and biting brand of humor that readers will continue to see in the novel. Finally, the warning is a convenient method by which to ward off literary critics who might be eager to dissect Twain's work. Twain recognizes, no doubt, that his novel will incite controversy.

Before the reader passes judgment on these warnings, perhaps a line or two from another of Twain's works, *Pudd'nhead Wilson,* will help put them in perspective: "Adam was but human—this explains it all. He did not want the apple for the apple's sake, he wanted it only because it was forbidden. The mistake was in not forbidding the serpent; then he would have eaten the serpent." (Pudd'head Wilson's Calendar, Chapter II.)

Chapter 1

Summary

The novel begins with Huck Finn introducing himself and referencing *The Adventures of Tom Sawyer*. "You don't know about me," Huck narrates, "without you have read a book by the name of "The Adventures of Tom Sawyer," but that ain't no matter." He tells readers that, for the most part, Twain told the truth in *Tom Sawyer* but that everyone tells some lies, even people like Aunt Polly and the Widow Douglas.

Huck gives a brief summary of how he and Tom got six thousand dollars each at the end of *Tom Sawyer*. Judge Thatcher has taken Huck's money and invested it with a dollar of interest coming in each day, and Huck now lives with the Widow Douglas and her sister, Miss Watson. The sisters are, as Huck puts it, trying to "sivilize" him, and his frustration at living in a clean house and minding his manners starts to grow. Miss Watson tells Huck he will go to "the bad place" if he does not behave, and Huck thinks that will be okay as long as Miss Watson is not there.

During the evening, Huck accidentally kills a spider that was on his shoulder and worries that bad luck will follow. When the town clock strikes twelve midnight, Huck hears a noise outside his window and climbs out to find Tom Sawyer waiting for him.

Commentary

The opening sentence of the novel notifies readers that Huck Finn is the narrator and will tell his story in his own words, in his own language and dialect (complete with grammatical errors and misspellings), and from his own point of view. By using the first person narrative point of view, Twain carries on the southwestern humor tradition of vernacular language; that is, Huck sounds as a young, uneducated boy from Missouri should sound.

This first sentence also alludes to *The Adventures of Tom Sawyer*. The allusion reminds the reader of a novel about boys and their adventures, the purpose of which, according to Twain, was to rekindle in adults memories "of how they felt and thought and talked, and what queer enterprises they sometimes engaged in." Then Huck—and Twain—dismiss the work with "But that ain't no matter." Although the boyish type adventure episodes tend to reappear as a plot motif in *Huck Finn*, especially in the sections including Tom, their primary purpose is more to communicate criticism of Twain's contemporary society than to evoke fond memories. This statement also makes clear that it does not matter whether readers have read Twain's earlier book or not. *Huck Finn* is Huck's story, and he will tell it from his natural, unsophisticated perspective.

Style & Language

This first chapter introduces several major literary elements. Humor is used in various ways in the novel, but Huck's deadpan narration and pragmatic personality juxtaposed to events and beliefs that make no logical or practical sense to him provide much of the novel's humor. Because Huck is young and uncivilized, he describes events and people in a direct manner without any extensive commentary. Huck does not laugh at humorous situations and statements simply because his literal approach does not find them to be funny; he fails to see the irony. He does not project social, religious, cultural, or conceptual nuances into situations because he has never learned them. For example, when Miss Watson tells Huck that "*she* was going to live so as to go to the good place [heaven]," Huck, applying what he knows about Miss Watson and the obvious lifestyle that makes her happy, responds that he "couldn't see no advantage in going where she was going," and makes up his mind to not try to get there. Huck does not intend his comment to be disrespectful or sarcastic; it is simply a statement of fact and is indicative of the literal, practical approach to life that he exhibits throughout the novel.

Theme

The first chapter also serves to introduce an important thematic image that pervades the work: natural, free individualism contrasted with the expectations of society. Huck feels confined by the social expectations of civilization and wants to return to his simple, carefree life. He dislikes the social and cultural trappings of clean clothes, Bible studies, spelling lessons, and manners that he is forced to follow. Huck cannot understand why people would want to live under such circumstances, and he longs to be able to return to his previous life where no one tries to "sivilize" him.

The contrast between freedom and civilization permeates the novel, and Huck's struggle for natural freedom (freedom from society) mirrors the more important struggle of Jim, who struggles for social freedom (freedom within the society). Both Huck and Jim search for freedom during their adventure down the Mississippi, and both find that civilization presents a large obstacle to obtaining their dream. From the beginning, readers realize that civilization is filled with certain hypocrisies, including religion and the practice of slavery.

Huck's candid narration gives Twain the opportunity to make barbed comments about literary and social institutions of the nineteenth century. The barbed comments range from his literary aversion to the novels of authors such as James Fenimore Cooper (*Last of the Mohicans*) to overt religious hypocrisies such as the Christian acceptance of slavery in his boyhood town.

Style & Language

The historical realities of slavery and racial division are, without doubt, the most important and most controversial elements in *Huck Finn*. Imbedded in the contrast between freedom and civilization is the issue of slavery, and the inclusion of the pejorative slang term "niggars" in the first chapter prepares readers for the similar coarse language that will follow. In order to depict the region and the attitude in a realistic manner, Twain makes a conscious choice not to edit regional bigotry and the language that accompanies it.

The reader should remain aware of two major points while reading this novel: First, the novel is a satire; that is, irony, sarcasm, or caustic wit are used to attack or expose folly, vice, or stupidity. Second, the novel is first person narrative (told from Huck's point of view). Confusing either of these issues can lead the unsophisticated reader to drastic misinterpretations. The feelings and interpretations of situations, issues, and events advanced by Huck are not necessarily those the author is advocating.

By the end of this first chapter, the reader has gathered a good deal of data about Huck: his mother is dead, his father is the town drunk, he has "a dollar a day . . . all the year round" income, he lacks "book learning," hates the "sivilized" ways, is keenly observant of details around him, and is a realist.

Glossary

sugar-hogshead a large barrel used to store sugar.

niggers niggar, originally a dialectal variant of *Negro*, the term is a derogatory and vulgar racial slur directed primarily toward African Americans.

Chapter 2

Summary

As Huck and Tom sneak off from the Widow Douglas' house, Huck trips, and the noise alerts Miss Watson's slave, Jim. Jim tries to find what made the noise and almost discovers the boys, but after a while he falls asleep. While Jim is sleeping, Tom takes Jim's hat and hangs it on a tree-limb. Afterwards, Jim tells everyone that witches put a spell on him and took him all over the state. Jim's story grows with each telling until finally slaves come from all over to hear Jim's tale of being bewitched. After this episode, he is considered an authority on witches.

Huck and Tom meet the rest of the town boys, and they all go to a hidden cave two miles down the river. In the cave, Tom declares that the band of robbers will be called "Tom Sawyer's Gang" and "Everybody that wants to join has got to take an oath, and write his name in blood." The boys all swear that, if a gang member tells the gang's secrets, they will cut his throat and then kill that boy's family. One of the boys says the oath is not fair because Huck Finn does not have a family unless you count a father who can never be found. A solution is found when Huck offers Miss Watson as his family and says, "they could kill her."

Using pirate books as a reference, Tom describes the future business of the gang as robbery and murder. The other boys wonder why everything must be so complicated and involve ransoms and guards, and Tom replies that he's "seen it in books; and so of course that's what we've got to do."

Commentary

Character Insight

Chapter 2 introduces Jim, Huck's future companion and friend. In Missouri, most slaves were domestic servants, not workers on plantations that most people today identify with slavery. Jim's initial behaviors as interpreted through Huck are stereotypical traits attributed to blacks at the time: laziness, a tendency toward exaggeration, and conceit. Jim's belief in superstition mirrors that of Huck, and his explanations of what had happened to him that night could be interpreted to reveal either a gullible nature or an opportunist who makes the most of the circumstances that he encounters. Twain not only taps Huck's prejudices in the early portrayal of Jim, but he also taps the prejudices of the reader. Jim gains handsomely from his witch adventure and wisely uses the fictional kidnapping to boost his stature among his peers. Nevertheless, the suggestion that Jim displays negative traits has been partially responsible for the opposition to teaching *Huck Finn* in the classroom.

The character of Jim, however, is much more complex than the sleepy man who has seen the devil and been kidnapped by witches. Moreover, this simplistic interpretation of Jim in the beginning of the novel enhances the prejudicial nature of the stereotype when the true depth of his character is revealed later in the novel. As readers learn about Huck, they also learn about Jim and the admirable character he is.

Literary Device

Also introduced in Chapter 2 is the character of Tom Sawyer. Tom is a contrasting character (a foil) to Huck, despite their obvious bond and friendship. Tom is a romantic, insensitive representative of the society Huck dislikes. His tendency is to take control, romanticize, and exaggerate all situations. Tom bases his expertise in adventures on the many pirate and robber books he has read. His humorous exaggerations symbolize Twain's dislike of popular and glorified romantic novels. Later, in Chapter 3, Tom mentions *Don Quixote* as a model of the romantic novels. Ironically, Cervantes was satirizing romantic adventure stories in this work much the same as Twain does in this work. Obviously, Tom was unaware of the satiric nature of the novel, but Twain was not.

Style & Language

Unlike the playful humor of Tom Sawyer, the humor of Huck Finn is bitter satire using the hypocrisy, violence, and squalor in the society that Twain observed. For example, when Tom decides that the gang will rob and murder people "except some that you bring to the cave here and keep them till they're ransomed," the boys discover that no one, including Tom, knows the meaning of "ransom." The boys assign a meaning to the word by conjecturing what it means ("keep them until they are dead"). This meaning, of course, is wrong, but, as in the greater society, because the group believes it to be true, it becomes their truth, and the rest of their action is based on this error, a serious subject matter undercut by humor.

Glossary

the quality word used by the South to describe aristocracy,

five-center piece monetary equivalent of a nickel. Nickels were not minted until after the Civil War.

skiff a flat-bottomed boat propelled by oars.

high-toned aristocratic or snobbish.

blame a milder slang alternative for "damned."

the nation slang for "damnation."

Chapter 3

Summary

The next day, Huck receives a scolding from Miss Watson because of his dirty clothes, but the Widow Douglas does not reproach him at all. Miss Watson explains to Huck that, through prayer, he can have anything he wants. She makes Huck pray for the next few days, and Huck does not understand why the fishhooks he prays for never arrive.

During this time, Huck is told that his father, Pap Finn, has been found drowned in the river. Because the body was floating on his back, the superstitious Huck does not believe it is Pap and worries that the violent Pap will show up again. The Tom Sawyer Gang disbands because the only adventure they have is attempting to rob a Sunday-school picnic.

Commentary

In Chapter 3, the practical Huck again struggles to understand religion. When Miss Watson tells Huck he can receive anything he wants through prayer, the literal Huck believes he can receive fishing gear. He contemplates the concept of prayer and wonders why, if someone can get anything, he cannot get any fish-hooks, the widow cannot reclaim her stolen silver snuff-box, and Miss Watson cannot "fat up"? The humorous moment is another example of Huck's literal approach to his surroundings. Because Huck takes everything at face value, he cannot understand the concept of prayer or "spiritual gifts." He does not reject religion, but his literal mindset has difficulty with beliefs that, on the surface, appear to be impractical or untrue.

More important, Huck's struggle compares and contrasts the religions of the Widow Douglas and Miss Watson as he begins to see that religion is practiced differently by his guardians. Through Huck, Twain is exploring his own reservations about religion and its ties to the institution of slavery. It is not incidental that it is Miss Watson who owns Jim and not the Widow Douglas, and Huck continues to question religion and the rules of his society. Huck eventually decides that there are two kinds of Providence, and he would like to avoid Miss Watson's and go to the one the Widow Douglas describes.

Chapter 3 continues to establish Tom and Huck as contrasting characters. Whereas Huck takes a literal approach to everything he sees and hears, Tom's knowledge comes solely from the books he reads. At the same time Huck questions religion, he begins to see Tom's "magicians and A-rabs" as fabrication. For Huck, Tom's imagination has the same quality as Miss Watson's religion, and he distrusts the superficial nature of both. This approach serves Huck well throughout the novel. Although he does not completely understand prayer, he does understand the widow's explanation that he "must help other people . . . and look out for them all the time, and never think about myself." By applying his own conscience and beliefs, Huck grows as a character and is able to form his own opinions and not blindly accept society's values and the status quo.

Glossary

hived robbed.

pow-wow to confer, to have an intense discussion; originally from a North American Indian word.

"sumter" mule sumpter mule, a packhorse, mule, or other animal used for carrying baggage.

lay in ambuscade hide in ambush.

slick up to polish.

tract a propagandizing pamphlet, especially one on a religious or political subject.

sap-head a fool.

Chapter 4

Summary

Three or four months have passed when Huck finds a suspicious footprint in the snow outside of the widow's house. Because of a cross carved in the heel, the print looks exactly like Pap Finn's boot, and Huck begins to worry that Pap has returned. To protect the reward money from Pap, Huck goes to see Judge Thatcher and tries to persuade Judge Thatcher to take the money for his own.

Because Jim is rumored to have the ability to do magic, Huck asks him if he can predict what Pap will do and where he will stay. When Huck asks Jim about Pap's plans, Jim places a hairball on the ground and listens for Huck's fortune. Jim says that there are two angels hovering over Pap—one white and one black—and he does not know which way Pap will decide to live his life. Jim also says that, just like Pap Finn, Huck has two angels over him, trying to help him decide the right path. When Huck returns to his room that night, he finds Pap waiting for him.

Commentary

When Pap's tracks appear, Huck would rather give his money away than risk confronting Pap. He knows that Pap is inspired only by whisky or greed, and if Huck is poor, perhaps Pap will leave him alone. In the previous chapter, Pap is described as a town vagrant who "used to lay drunk with the hogs in the tanyard" and Huck is not affected by the description. But Huck's indifference to Pap's reputation changes when he realizes Pap is back in town. Huck's fear is understated, but it suggests that his previous life with Pap was violent and dysfunctional. Moreover, the subtle threat of abuse underscores the theme of a chaotic and violent environment after the Civil War, an environment that Huck cannot entirely avoid despite his plans and cunning.

Literary Device

Chapter 4 continues to document that Huck and Jim are superstitious and are products of their society and their circumstances. When Jim uses the hairball to discover Pap's intentions, Jim ends up forecasting Huck's future more than Pap's, and the similarities between the two are obvious. According to Jim, both Pap and Huck have "two angels hoverin'" over them, and the future is uncertain. Jim warns Huck to stay away from the water because it is his fate to be hanged. The darkness in Huck's future, then, relates directly to the Mississippi River, and it is predestined ("down in de bills") that Huck will suffer because of it. The inclusion of predestination reflects Twain's Calvinist background. More important, however, the battle of the two angels foreshadows Huck's future battle with his conscience in terms of Jim's freedom.

Glossary

irish potato the common white potato; so called because extensively cultivated in Ireland.

down in de bills predestined, foreordained by divine decree or intent.

Chapters 5 and 6

Summary

That evening, Huck discovers Pap in his room. After the initial shock, Huck decides Pap is too disheveled to be a threat. Pap's hair is "long and tangled and greasy," his face is extremely pale, and his clothes are in rags. Pap immediately notices how clean Huck is in comparison and then begins a tirade about Huck attending school and trying to be more of a man than his father.

Over the next few days, Pap tries to get Huck's money from Judge Thatcher and gain custody of Huck. Pap is unable to get any money, except when he takes a dollar or two directly from Huck. Although the widow wants to raise Huck, Pap convinces a new judge that he has changed and will start a life free from alcohol and sin. The new judge decides that "he'd druther not take a child away from its father" and grants custody to Pap. The new judge finally realizes he has been taken for a fool, however, when Pap sneaks out and breaks his arm after getting "drunk as a fiddler."

Instead of avoiding school, Huck attends just to spite Pap. When the widow tells Pap to stop loitering around her house, Pap kidnaps Huck and takes him upriver to the Illinois shore. The widow discovers Huck's location and sends a man to rescue him, but Pap drives the man off with a gun.

After a couple of months, Pap's beatings become too harsh and too frequent, and Huck decides to escape. The same night as Huck's decision, Pap gets extremely drunk and begins to denounce the government for its laws and the positive treatment of African-Americans. Eventually both Pap and Huck fall asleep, and Huck wakes up to find Pap screaming about snakes and calling Huck the "Angel of Death."

Commentary

Upon discovering Pap, Huck's first thoughts are of the beatings that Pap used to give him. When Huck sees Pap's appearance, however, he immediately is put at ease. Pap's disheveled appearance does not frighten Huck; instead, Pap appears as a clown or buffoon with exaggerated features. The appearance is similar to other exaggerated frontier characters in American humor, but Pap is more than a caricature; he is the most evil character in the novel, and he is white, "a white to make a body sick, a white to make a body's flesh crawl."

Pap's threats are humorous because of the obvious irony; how could a father not be proud of his son learning to read? But as in Chapter 4, the threats are laced with the realization that Huck has been beaten by Pap before. Huck stays captive for the next couple of months and begins to enjoy his old life, free from manners, education, and religion. Huck's "free" life with Pap, however, comes at the price of physical abuse.

Theme

Pap's miserable character represents yet another negative element of society. Pap exudes bigotry and hate. His ludicrous tirade against the government and blacks is pathetically comical because of his obvious arrogance and ignorance and the slapstick humor involved in Huck's description. The irony, however, is more painful than it is humorous because it symbolizes a common racist attitude built on ignorance and insecurity.

Literary Device

When Pap calls Huck the Angel of Death at the end of Chapter 6, the name appears to be one of Pap's hallucinations. The label is important, however, and foreshadows the numerous deaths that Huck encounters as he escapes down the Mississippi.

Glossary

black slouch　a felt hat with a broad, floppy rim.

put in her shovel　offered an opinion.

pungle　to pay.

bullyragged　scolded, chastised.

forty-rod　cheap whisky.

tow　a rope made from strands of broken or coarse flax or hemp.

mulatter　mulatto, a person who has one black parent and one white parent.

habob　aristocratic member of the community.

delirium tremens　involuntary muscle spasm usually associate with drinking alcohol and characterized by sweating, anxiety, and hallucinations.

Chapter 7

Summary

The next day Huck finds a drifting canoe on the rising river. When Pap leaves for the night to go drinking, Huck escapes through a hole he sawed in the cabin wall. He takes all the cabin's supplies and puts them in the canoe; he then shoots a wild hog and uses its blood to make it look as if he were murdered. By staging his own murder, Huck thinks he can escape without the threat of being followed. At dark, he leaves in the canoe and eventually lands downstream at Jackson's Island.

Commentary

Theme

Twain gives the readers another literary glimpse of the river that enchanted him throughout his life and career. The quiet Mississippi quickly lulls Huck to sleep. The river becomes symbolic of Huck's more peaceful, natural life. The description is important, because it underscores the serenity of the river and of nature in general as opposed to the harsh and chaotic world on shore. Throughout the novel, Twain continues to outline the difference between the two worlds, and the juxtaposition of the peaceful river and brutal shore has often been described as the "raft/shore dichotomy."

Huck's flight shows his creativity and cleverness, but it also establishes a logical method of escape. Every action Huck performs, from placing blood on an axe to dragging a bag full of meal, is practical and works to help his plan. The escape is efficient, and although Huck wishes Tom were there to "throw in the fancy touches," readers realize that Tom's additions would create more problems than solutions. Huck's practicality is evident not only in his narrative reaction to events but also in his physical actions. The self-reliant characteristic aids Huck well in the future, as he faces decisions that require individual thought and rejection of accepted beliefs.

Glossary

palavering talking or idly chattering.

trot line a strong fishing line suspended ove the water, with short, baited lines hung at intervals.

slough a place, as a hollow, full of soft, deep mud; a swamp, bog, or marsh, especially one that is part of an inlet or backwater.

stabbord starboard, the right side of a ship or boat or boat as one faces forward.

Chapter 8

Summary

Huck wakes up on Jackson's Island to hear a ferryboat firing a cannon. He knows that this will bring a drowned body to the surface and realizes that they must be searching for him. Huck also remembers that another way to find a body is with a loaf of bread filled with quicksilver. He scouts the shoreline and finds a large loaf, then wonders if prayer really works. Someone, after all, had prayed that the bread find his body, and that prayer had worked.

Confident that he is now safe, Huck explores the island until he stumbles upon fresh campfire ashes. Huck climbs a tree for safety but curiosity sends him back to the site, and he discovers Miss Watson's slave, Jim. After convincing Jim that he is not a ghost, Huck learns that Jim has run away because Miss Watson was going to sell him down the river to New Orleans.

During the evening, Jim impresses Huck with his knowledge of superstition.

Commentary

Character Insight

Huck's contemplation of prayer brims with humor as he tries to fathom the logic of how the quicksilver bread found him. The combination of a superstitious practice (quicksilver bread) and a religious custom (prayer) shows that Huck's beliefs include a portion of both. As reluctant as he is to embrace Miss Watson's religion, he still holds a fearful respect of its power. The same is true for the practice of superstition.

When Huck first stumbles upon Jim, he does not immediately ask why Jim is on the island, nor does he worry that Jim will tell anyone he is alive. Instead, Huck's first reaction is one of joy at the companionship. More important, Jim's reintroduction extends the important theme of freedom and civilization from Huck to Jim, and sets up the circumstances that will lead to their odyssey down the Mississippi.

Huck's continued struggle with society's restrictions and laws now includes the more serious issue of race and slavery. Huck's comment that "people would call me a low-down Abolitionist and despise me for keeping mum" shows that his society does not tolerate those who denounce slavery. This is Huck's first important break with society, but a break that would make his return nearly impossible, as he realizes. The stance is similar to Twain's own boyhood experience where slavery was an accepted practice in the South. Although Huck has shown the tendency to reject society's beliefs, he cannot immediately dismiss its influence and teachings.

Literary Device

This chapter also serves to establish the relationship between Huck and Jim and their roles in contrast to one another. Whereas Huck's initial representation of Jim was stereotypical, in this chapter, Jim quickly reveals himself as an authority on superstition. Huck's literal nature does not allow him to be impressed easily, but his belief in signs and superstition elevates Jim, who "knowed all kinds." In addition, Twain was fond of using a twin image in order to develop his themes. In some works the image is obvious (for example, *Pudd'nhead Wilson* and *The Prince and the Pauper*). In others, the image is more subtle. In this work, Tom and Huck are twins with differing dominate personality characteristics: Tom, the romantic, and Huck, the realist. Likewise, Jim and Huck are twin-like, each searching for his own kind of freedom, but one black, the other white.

Glossary

corn-pone corn meal.

sand in my craw courage.

fan-tods the nervous fidgets.

plug er dog-leg a plug of cheap chewing tobacco.

taller tallow, the nearly colorless solid fat extracted from the natural fat of cattle or sheep, used in making candles and soaps.

Chapters 9 and 10

Summary

After exploring Jackson's Island, Jim and Huck find a cavern to hide in high on a steep ridge. They hide the canoe and then haul their traps and supplies up to the cavern. Huck thinks the location is too difficult to reach, but Jim argues that it will help protect them against people and the rain. Just as Jim predicted in Chapter 8, a large storm comes.

The river rises for 10 or 12 days, and the flooding waters give Jim and Huck the opportunity to explore and capture useful debris. One night, they discover a two-story frame house drifting along. Inside the house, Jim sees a dead man and instructs Huck not to look at the dead man's face because " . . . it's too gashly." Avoiding the body, they search the house and find an "old speckled straw hat," among the clothes, bottles, and other household items.

Back at the cavern, Huck tries to get Jim to discuss the dead man, but Jim avoids the subject saying it would bring bad luck and the man could "ha'nt us." They search the odds and ends they took from the floating house and discover eight dollars in an overcoat.

Because of the money and supplies, Huck argues that they are having good luck despite what Jim has told him. Later, Huck tries to play a prank on Jim and places a dead rattlesnake at the foot of Jim's blanket. When Jim lies down to sleep, the snake's mate is there and bites him. Jim is sick for several days and uses Pap's whisky to kill the pain of the snakebite. Eventually, he regains his strength, and Huck realizes the danger of defying superstition and Jim's expertise.

After a few days, Huck and Jim decide to sneak into town to learn of any news. Huck disguises himself as a girl and goes to the shanty of a woman he does not know.

Commentary

Character Insight

Jim's ability to predict the storm is an understated but important moment in the novel. As readers are aware, Pap Finn does not fulfill the role of father or parent except when it is convenient to Pap. In contrast, Jim's protective and caring nature is clear throughout the novel.

An example of Jim's parental role is when he does not allow Huck to view the face of the body on the floating house. The motion is subtle, but the protective action is more apparent later in the last chapter of the novel when readers learn that the dead man is Pap.

Literary Device

With the discovery of the dead man, Huck's earlier label as the "Angel of Death" comes into play again in Chapters 9 and 10. Despite the fabrications of death and the superstitions surrounding it, Huck does not confront death until he and Jim discover the body inside the house. Huck's initial reluctance is replaced by a strong curiosity with the man and the events that caused his demise. "I couldn't keep from studying over it wishing I knowed who shot the man, and what they done it for," Huck says.

Character Insight

In contrast to Jim's protective nature, Huck plays the first of three failed pranks directed at Jim. Despite his respect for Jim's knowledge of superstition, Huck still acts in a careless and impractical manner, and the first prank results in Jim's snakebite. Huck's regret at the outcome demonstrates the growth of his character and indicates that Huck does value Jim as a companion and a friend. This value, however, is pitted against Huck's belief that he should turn Jim in to authorities. The result is a constant clash between Huck's feelings of admiration and friendship for Jim and his fear of being judged for helping a runaway slave.

Glossary

Barlow knife a jackknife with one blade.

two bits 25 cents.

reticule a small handbag or sewing bag, orginally made of needlework and usually having a drawstring.

curry-comb a metal comb.

peart pert, lively, chipper, or smart.

Chapter 11

Summary

Still in disguise, Huck enters the woman's house and introduces himself as "Sarah Williams from Hookerville." Accepting Huck as a girl, the woman talks freely about the town's events and eventually reaches the subject of Huck and Tom, the reward money, and Huck's "murder." Suspicion began with Pap Finn, she says, but after Jim escaped, the town decided that the runaway slave had murdered Huck. With both Pap and Jim still suspects, the town has announced a reward of $300 for Jim and $200 for Pap.

The woman tells Huck she thinks she knows where Jim could be hiding, for she is sure she has seen smoke over at Jackson's Island. Huck becomes nervous when he learns that the woman's husband and another man are heading for Jackson's Island to search for Jim. Before Huck can leave, the woman figures out that he is not a girl, and Huck makes up yet another wild tale for explanation.

Huck rushes back to Jackson's Island and wakes Jim with the news that "There ain't a minute to lose. They're after us!" In complete silence, the two runaways pack their camp and head down the river on the raft.

Commentary

Chapter 11 displays yet another facet of *Huck Finn's* humor; that is, the ability of Huck to disguise himself and convince gullible adults to believe his preposterous stories. Huck is, indeed, an imaginative trickster who lies and fibs his way along the Mississippi. (These traits are one reason that authors such as Louisa May Alcott condemned his character as being unsuitable for young readers.) Huck is also prone, however, to forget his early stories, and therefore he is forced to invent new tales in order to continue his deception. The constantly changing fabrication is certainly comical and displays the creative ability of Huck as well as the ignorance of the people he meets.

The fact that the woman fools Huck into revealing his identity as a boy also provides much of the humor in the chapter. Despite his maverick nature, Huck is a product of the environment and thus is subject to the same type of manipulation that he performs on others. The tricks that the woman uses force Huck to reveal his male nature, his "boy" characteristics (the inability to thread a needle, for example). Even though the woman discovers Huck is not a girl, Huck is still able to save his story by donning another disguise as an orphaned and mistreated apprentice. The added story is yet another example of Huck's ability to succeed and adapt in a world of scams and con artists.

The readers should note that Chapter 11 ends with Huck and Jim functioning as a team. When Huck discovers that Jim is in danger, he does not think about society's judgment and simply reacts. In Huck's view, the pursuing men are after both of them, even though the consequences for Huck would be minimal. In other words, Huck unconsciously places Jim's safety above his own, and their separate struggles for freedom become one. As Huck and Jim slip "past the foot of the island dead still, never saying a word," Twain takes another step away from the childish adventures of *Tom Sawyer* and cements the relationship between the two outcasts.

Chapters 12 and 13

Summary

Jim and Huck continue down the river between the Missouri mountains and the "heavy timber" of Illinois, hiding the raft during the day and running several hours at night. The fifth night after they pass St. Louis, they come upon a steamboat crippled on a rock. Although Jim does not want to board the wreck and argues that they should ignore it, Huck convinces him that they need to explore.

On board, they overhear voices and see that two men have tied up a third and are discussing his fate. Certain that the wreck will come loose and sink, the two men decide to leave the tied man to a watery death. When Jim tries to untie the men's skiff and trap them on the wreck, he discovers the raft has broken loose and floated away. While the men are inside the cabin, Huck and Jim take the skiff and leave the wreck. Eventually they find the raft and pull the skiff and the men's supplies up on the deck.

When they come upon a village, Huck finds a ferryboat watchman and begins another elaborate story. He tells him that his family is up on the steamboat wreck, which readers learn is named the *Walter Scott*. The man hurries off to sound the alarm with visions of a reward in front of him.

Later that evening, Huck sees the wreck, which has come loose from the rocks and is quietly sinking as it drifts down the river.

Commentary

Twain's decision to name the boat the *Walter Scott* continues his mockery of romantic novels and their authors. The wreck's importance to the novel, however, is found in the contrasting images of peace and brutality and Huck's inevitable deliberations on death.

Chapter 12 signals a separation from Huck and Jim's familiar surroundings as the two begin their journey down the Mississippi. The peaceful images of the river are similar to those that readers have seen in the many film adaptations of *Huck Finn*: Huck and Jim on a large and comfortable raft, free from outside interference and enjoying the serenity of their new life. Although the river is seen as a safe haven for Huck and Jim, the viciousness of the shore arrives in the form of the *Walter Scott* wreck. In this manner, Twain is able to interrupt the peaceful environment of the river by combining it with the brutality of men. The pattern is one that will recur when the duke and the king board the raft in Chapter 19.

Despite their savageness and unfeeling attitude, Huck cannot help but "worry about the men" as he leaves them to die. Huck's compassion is evident, and he does attempt to save the men by alerting the ferryboat watchman. The "Angel of Death," however, claims more victims as the *Walter Scott* breaks apart and sinks.

Glossary

tow-head sandbar with thick reeds.

harrow-teeth wood or metal spikes used to plow land.

mushmelon a cantaloupe or other moderate sized melon.

jackstaff an iron rod or wooden bar on a ship to which the sails are fastened.

Sir Walter Scott (1771-1832) Scottish poet and novelist, author of *Ivanhoe*.

Chapter 14

Summary

The next day, Jim and Huck go through the spoils they got from the gang on the *Walter Scott*. Huck's excitement about their new treasure is tempered by Jim's fear that they might have been caught or drowned. After listening to Jim, Huck realizes that, as usual, Jim is right.

Among the blankets, clothes, and cigars, Huck finds a few books and reads to Jim about romantic figures like kings, dukes, and earls. When the discussion turns to royalty and King Solomon, Huck and Jim debate Solomon's logic and refuse to agree on his wisdom.

Commentary

Character Insight

Chapter 14 continues to define Huck and Jim's roles, with Jim constantly proving himself as the more practical and mature person despite Huck's ability to read. Initially, Huck accepts Jim's rationale when he describes why the *Walter Scott* presented so much danger. Huck's admission that " . . . he [Jim] was most always right" is undercut, however, by his statement that Jim " . . . had an uncommon level head, for a nigger." The vulgar label—which, of course, Huck does not recognize as vulgar—shows that Huck still has not accepted Jim as an intellectual or human equal, in spite of the fact that Jim continues to show superior logic, and Huck continues to grow fonder of him.

Literary Device

When the two discuss King Solomon, Jim's practical but single-minded approach cannot convince Huck that Solomon "*warn't* no wise man nuther." Readers, however, are able to see that it is Huck, and not Jim, who misses the point. The real point, as Jim says, "is down furder —it's down deeper." The statement foreshadows the debate of conscience that Huck undergoes later in the novel.

Glossary

the texas a structure on the hurricane deck of a steamboat, containing the officers' quarters, etc. and having the pilothouse on top or in front.

dauphin the eldest son of the king of France, a title used from 1349 to 1830.

polly-voo franzy parlez-vous Francais, "Do you speak French?"

Chapters 15 and 16

Summary

Jim and Huck believe that three more nights will bring them to Cairo, Illinois, and, from that point, they can take a steamboat up the Ohio River to the free states. On the second night, however, a dense fog rolls in, and the strong current separates Huck and Jim. After calling in vain for Jim, Huck decides to take "one little cat-nap" and wakes up several hours later under a clear sky.

He eventually finds Jim, who is in tears over seeing Huck again. Instead of celebrating their reunion, Huck decides to act as if Jim has been dreaming and Huck has been on the raft the entire night. Jim's concern turns to confusion, but he finally realizes Huck is lying. He admonishes Huck for the prank and says that only "trash" would treat a friend like that. After a few minutes, Huck feels so ashamed that he apologizes to Jim.

Jim and Huck decide that Huck must go ashore to check their progress. Jim's excitement is obvious, and Huck struggles with his shame of helping a slave escape. When Jim says he will steal his children out of slavery if necessary, Huck decides he must go ashore and turn Jim in to the authorities. Instead of rushing ashore at dawn to free his conscience, however, Huck covers for Jim when he runs into townspeople.

Shortly after, Huck and Jim see the clear water of the Ohio River and realize they have passed Cairo in the fog. They decide to buy another canoe to head upriver, but a steamboat wrecks the raft and the two are once again separated.

Commentary

Before 1991, critics largely believed that Twain stopped writing after Chapter 16 and set the manuscript aside. The assertion appears logical, for Cairo is, indeed, the original destination of Jim and Huck. If Huck and Jim make it to Cairo, they can head north up the Ohio River, and the story heads toward its conclusion. It is obvious that Twain was struggling with the novel's direction, but the 1991 discovery of the first half of the *Huck Finn* manuscript revealed that Twain had continued through Chapter 18 and then set aside the manuscript for two years.

Although Huck is distraught at the thought of losing Jim, he does play the horrible prank, which contrasts sharply with Jim's parental demeanor. Tom Sawyer, no doubt, would have been proud of Huck's creativity and imagination, but Huck realizes that he has done more than embarrass Jim; he has taken advantage of his trust and friendship. The elaborate joke wounds Jim, and Huck is not prepared for Jim's confession that his "heart wuz mos' broke bekase you wuz los', en I didn' k'yer no' mo' what become er me en de raf'." Jim's somber comment serves, in a sense, to break the heart of Huck, and readers realize, just as Huck does, that Jim would give his life for the young boy who has always been on the opposite side of societal laws.

Character Insight

Huck's comment that it took him 15 minutes to apologize is overshadowed only by the fact that he actually does. In Jim and Huck's squalid world, an apology from a white person to a slave is not only unnecessary, it is scandalous. Huck, however, does not regret his decision to apologize and learns another lesson about Jim's loyalty. He does not play another prank on Jim, but he continues to feel guilt over helping a slave. The irony of the situation is painful, as Huck condemns himself for protecting Jim instead of recognizing the heroics involved.

By passing Cairo, Twain is able to navigate the familiar setting of the Mississippi River and the South. The passage down-river also allows Huck to continue his battle between his instincts and what society dictates he should do. Despite his shame from the prank, Huck still struggles with his conscience. His decision to turn Jim in details the twisted logic of slavery that condemns a man for wanting to rescue his children from captivity. The biting satire is obvious, as is the realization that Huck cannot defy society's moral code of racism without a struggle. He is, after all, resisting all the social and cultural reasoning that made slavery possible.

Theme

When the two men searching for runaway slaves surprise Huck, however, he develops an elaborate story that saves Jim. Once again Huck's actions mirror his natural conscience. Huck is constantly pulled between what he is supposed to think and feel (that is, what he has been taught either by lessons or social example) and what he actually feels and thinks (that is, what he has developed through his personal and natural experiences). He finds himself aiding Jim, who grows more certain of Huck's loyalty and friendship.

Glossary

Cairo city in southern Illinois, at the confluence of the Ohio and Mississippi Rivers.

buckle to paddle hard.

Muddy the Mississippi River.

Chapters 17 and 18

Summary

Once on shore, Huck finds himself at an impressive log house owned by the Grangerford family. After they are convinced that Huck is not a member of the Shepherdson family, the Grangerfords take Huck in, give him warm clothes, and feed him. Huck tells everyone that his name is George Jackson and that he fell off a passing steamboat.

The Grangerfords have a son named Buck, who is about Huck's age, and the two become close friends over the next few days. Huck admires the stately house with its large fireplaces, ornate door locks, and elaborate decor. The morbid paintings and poetry of Emmeline, a deceased daughter of the Grangerfords, also fascinate him.

Huck soon learns that the Grangerfords share a steamboat landing with another aristocratic family named Shepherdson. When Huck and Buck go hunting, Buck takes a shot at young Harney Shepherdson and misses. While the boys run away, Huck notices that Harney has a chance to shoot Buck but rides away instead. Huck wonders about Harney but finally decides he was going after his hat. In response to Huck's questions, Buck explains that the Grangerfords and Shepherdsons have been feuding for so long that no one remembers why it began in the first place.

After Huck delivers a message for Sophia Grangerford, he is taken over to the swamp by one of the family's many slaves. Among the trees, Huck finds Jim, who says that he has found the raft. The next day, Miss Sophia elopes with Harney Shepherdson. The bizarre feud escalates, and several men on both sides of the family are killed, including Buck. Huck regrets ever coming ashore and cannot tell us "all that happened" because it would make him sick to do so. He rejoins Jim, and the two decide a raft is the best home.

Commentary

The introduction of the Grangerfords and Shepherdsons adds a new element of humor to Twain's novel. Whereas earlier Twain satirizes the actions of "common" townspeople, the stately families provide a perfect opportunity for Twain to burlesque the Southern code of chivalry and aristocracy of the antebellum South. The Grangerford's house represents a gaudy and tasteless display of wealth, and Huck's appreciation of the decor only adds to the humor. The decor that exemplifies the Grangerford's taste is the artistic work of Emmeline, the deceased daughter who pined away after failing to discover a rhyme for "Whistler." In contrast to Huck's practical fascination with death, Emmeline's work displays a romantic and sentimental obsession that even gives Huck the "fantods."

Literary Device

Twain also uses the families to underscore his subtle satire on religion, as the two families attend the same church, leaning their guns against the walls during the sermon about "brotherly love." The mixture of theology and gunplay is ironic, as is the family's subsequent reaction that the sermon was filled with positive messages about "faith and good work and free grace and preforeordestination." Twain's Calvinist background resurfaces in his combination of predestination and foreordination.

Theme

The feud between the Grangerfords and Shepherdsons is one of the more memorable chapters in *Huck Finn* because of its extreme violence. The fact that the two noble families do not know why they continue to fight is ironic, but the irony deepens when the families actually draw blood. Huck's casual observance turns into participation, and when he witnesses the death of his young friend, Buck, he is unable to recount the story to readers. The hated calls of "Kill them, kill them!" prompt Huck to wish that he had never gone ashore, despite his affection for the Grangerfords. The theme of death and brutality, then, is present in all facets of society, including the wealthy, and the peace of the river is never more apparent to Huck.

When Huck returns to the raft and he and Jim are safe, Huck wearily observes that " . . . there warn't no home like a raft, after all . . .. You feel mighty free and easy and comfortable on a raft." The unaffected statement solidifies the raft/shore dichotomy and reinforces the idea that society, despite its sophistication, is cruel and unjust.

Glossary

dog-irons iron braces used to hold firewood.

Pilgrim's Progress a religious allegory by John Bunyan (1678).

mud-cat a catfish.

liberty-pole a tall flagstaff planted in the ground.

bowie a steel knife about fifteen inches long, with a single edge, usually carried in a sheath.

nip and tuck so close that the outcome is uncertain.

predestination the theological doctrine that God foreordained everything that would happen.

foreordination predestination.

puncheon floor floor made of a heavy, broad piece of roughly dressed timber with one side hewed flat.

Chapters 19 and 20

Summary

After two or three peaceful days on the raft, Huck is searching for some berries in a creek when he comes upon two desperate men. The men are obviously being chased, and Huck tells them how to lose the dogs, and they escape. The men, one around 70 and the other around 30 years old, join Huck and Jim on the raft.

Each man quickly discovers that they both are con artists, and they decide to work together. Shortly after their agreement, the youngest breaks into tears and claims that he is the Duke of Bridgewater and must be treated with respect. After a thoughtful moment, the oldest uses the same tactic and claims to be the Dauphin, the rightful heir to the French throne. Huck believes the men are simple con men but decides not to challenge them in order to keep the peace.

The duke and the king begin scheming, and with new plans, they land the raft below the one-horse town of Pokeville, which is practically deserted because of a nearby camp meeting. When the duke heads off to find a printing shop, the king decides to attend the meeting. At the meeting, the townspeople sing hymns and go up to the pulpit for forgiveness. The king joins the festivities and professes to be an old pirate who has reformed and seen the errors of his past. He burst into tears and passes around his hat and collects $87 dollars and a jug of whisky.

When they return to the raft, Huck and Jim find that the duke has printed a handbill that describes Jim as a runaway slave from New Orleans. The handbill, the duke argues, will allow them to run the raft during the day without intrusion. The next morning, Jim says he can abide one or two kings but no more than that.

Commentary

Chapter 19 continues to outline the carefree and unaffected environment aboard the raft. The days pass "smooth and lovely," and Twain uses the opportunity to portray the beauty of the Mississippi and its natural surroundings. During this time, Huck's narrative is filled with calm images of approaching dawn, small breezes, hot breakfasts, and a sky "speckled with stars."

Theme

The peaceful environment of the raft is shattered by the arrival of the duke and the king. At this point, the raft, which has been a kind of sanctuary, is invaded by society. The two men symbolize the stark contrast of the river to the shore and once again outline the raft/shore dichotomy. In a larger sense, the duke and the king represent the confidence men that roamed both the urban and rural landscape of nineteenth-century America, always attempting to prey on the gullible and naive. The confidence man of early frontier literature used not only society's vices but also its convictions and trust to employ his schemes, and the duke and the king exemplify the trickster who takes advantage of an ignorant society.

Character Insight

At first, the men appear harmless, and Huck quietly rejects their preposterous claims of royalty. Huck's gesture of kindness is similar to his compassion for the doomed men aboard the *Walter Scott*, but he quickly realizes the danger that the frauds present. His recognition of their true character is important, for he understands that the two pose a particular threat to Jim. Huck's insight, however, is not surprising, for the men are simply exaggerations of the characters that Huck and Jim have already encountered during their journey. Huck has learned that society is not to be trusted, and the duke and the king quickly show that his concern is legitimate.

The inclusion of the camp meeting is a perfect example of the confidence man. Along with its playful burlesque of religion, the camp meeting shows a gullible audience that is swindled because of its faith. The ensuing scene is reminiscent of George Washington Harris' "Sut Lovingood's Lizards" and Johnson J. Hooper's "Simon Suggs Attends a Camp Meeting." Both authors were influential for Twain and reflect a society that is scammed because of its misplaced faith or hypocrisy.

Glossary

gar needlefish.

galoot [Slang] a person, esp. an awkward, ungainly person.

carpet-bag an old-fashioned type of traveling bag, made of carpeting.

tar and feather to cover a person with tar and feathers as in punishment by mob action.

mesmerism hypnotism.

bilgewater water that collects in the bilge of a ship, slang for worthless or silly talk.

tick a cloth case covering that is filled with cotton, feathers, or hair to form a mattress or pillow.

gingham a yarn-dyed cotton cloth, usually woven in stripes, checks, or plaids.

calico a printed cotton fabric.

camp-meeting here, a religious revival.

Chapters 21, 22, and 23

Summary

Preparing for their next scam, the duke and king practice the balcony scene from *Romeo and Juliet* and the sword fight from *Richard III*. As an encore, the duke also teaches the king a jumbled version of *Hamlet*'s soliloquy. A few days later, they go ashore in Arkansas and decide to display their knowledge of Shakespeare. The town is a squalid place with streets of mud and loafers spitting tobacco. As Huck explores, a drunken man named Boggs races into town vowing to kill a man named Colonel Sherburn. The local townspeople laugh at Boggs and remark that his behavior is common practice, and he is harmless. After a brief period, Sherburn comes out of his office and tells Boggs to stop speaking out against him. Boggs continues to swear at Sherburn, and, in retaliation, Sherburn levels a pistol and kills him.

The town immediately decides that Sherburn must be lynched, and they storm to his house in an angry mob. When they arrive, Sherburn greets them from the roof of his porch and stands up to the mob. The crowd quickly disperses after Sherburn calls them cowards and declares they do not have the "grit enough" to confront a real man.

After the Shakespearean Revival fails to bring in any significant money, the duke and king advertise a show where no women and children are allowed. Unable to resist, several men show up for the first show to find the king on stage, naked and painted with colorful stripes. The men soon realize they have been scammed, but instead of revealing their ignorance to the rest of the town, they convince the other townsmen to attend the show. After two successive scams, the townsmen arrive at the third show with plans to tar and feather the duke and king. While the men prepare to barrage the stage with rotten vegetables, the duke sneaks out with Huck, and they join the king and Jim and leave the town.

Commentary

As with the satire of the camp meeting, the parody of Shakespeare is another staple of frontier humor that Twain uses for comic effect. The duke's version includes a mixture of *Hamlet* and *Macbeth*, and the resulting soliloquy contains misplaced phrases such as "To be, or not to be; that is the bare bodkin."

Literary Device

The irony of the two frauds attempting to quote Shakespeare is surpassed only by the irony of their attempt to present it to the small Arkansas village. Huck's description of the barren town and its inhabitants reminds readers of the squalid and cruel nature of society. The men are not only cruel to defenseless animals, they are also vicious with one another as is revealed in the death of poor Boggs. Similar to Twain's use of the Mississippi, the murder of Boggs is based on a real event that Twain witnessed as a young man. The incident illustrates the dangers of pride and a mob mentality, and also symbolizes human's contempt for one another. The fact that Boggs' earlier actions are deemed harmless further illustrates that no one in Huck's world is immune from corruption and hatred.

Character Insight

The cruelty of the Boggs episode is easily recognized by Huck, as is the general squalor of the town. Huck's reaction is noteworthy, for it contrasts sharply with the "evils" of his companion, Jim. Among the string of characters that Huck encounters—from Pap to the Grangerfords to Sherburn—Jim stands above them despite society's condemnation. Huck's inability to transcend his environment and give way to his instincts forces him to struggle with Jim's plight. Even in comparison to the disorder and injustice of the towns and their inhabitants, Huck still cannot reconcile his abolitionist actions and Jim's freedom. Huck's character further matures as he watches Jim mourn for his wife and children because he misses them. Huck observes that blacks possibly love their families as much as whites love theirs. Huck's observation underscores the depth of ignorance and bigotry exhibited in a society that does not believe blacks to be as capable of strong emotions as whites.

The King's Campelopard and the Royal Nonesuch are based upon degrading and bawdy humor, and thus they are appropriate for the townsmen. As mentioned earlier, the strategy of the confidence man is to play upon the virtues and vices of society. By appealing to the base nature of the men, the duke and the king are able to lure them into their scam and then escape before retaliation.

Glossary

Capet Hugh Capet, king of France (987-996); here, the duke's reference to the king.

jimpson weed jimson weed; a poisonous annual weed (Datura stramonium) of the nightshade family, with foul-smelling leaves, prickly fruit, and white or purplish, trumpet-shaped flowers.

sold scammed, to be made a fool

Chapter 24

Summary

The next day, the duke paints Jim's face solid blue so they can navigate the river during the day. To complete the disguise, the duke posts a sign on the raft reading "Sick Arab—but harmless when not out of his head."

The two con men decide to scout the surrounding towns, and while the king and Huck are heading to the steamboat, they pick up a young boy in their canoe. The king questions the talkative boy thoroughly about the town and discovers a local man, Peter Wilks, has just died and left all his fortune to his English brothers.

After learning the details of the Wilks family and its friends, the king sends Huck to fetch the duke, and the con men pose as Peter Wilks' English brothers, Harvey and William. They enter the town and begin to cry and moan when they hear of their "brothers" death. The cruel approach of the scam surprises even Huck, and he comments that "it was enough to make a body ashamed of the human race."

Commentary

The events of Chapter 24 reveal that the duke and the king have taken complete control of the raft and its travelers. The fact that the duke unties Jim and uses a disguise to give him freedom during the day is overshadowed by the latest ploy to inherit a dead man's fortune.

Similar to their earlier methods that played off of faith and conviction, the duke and the king plot to earn the confidence of an entire town. The task becomes ludicrous when readers realize that the duke and king must convince everyone of their English heritage and that William (the duke) is "deef and dumb." The humor of the con men's upcoming scam is apparent, as is the realization that this plot is more callous than their previous pranks. Twain's burlesque on the ignorance of humankind is evident, for to succeed, the con men need a community of fools.

Theme

Huck's somber observation that "it was enough to make a body ashamed of the human race" alerts readers that he has again been forced to evaluate his society. Whereas earlier events took place with little judgment, the Wilks scam, coupled with the death of Buck Grangerford, forces Huck to condemn the entire race. The statement underscores Huck's constant struggle.

Chapters 25 and 26

Summary

The king and the duke put on a dramatic display and convince the family and most of the town that they are, indeed, Wilks' brothers. Sobbing, they greet Peter Wilks' daughters as their nieces and cry over the coffin. The king gives a speech that, according to Huck, is "all full of tears and flapdoodle."

Peter Wilks' will gives all of his possessions to his brothers and divides $6,000 in gold among the daughters and Harvey and William. In order to cement the confidence of the town, the duke and the king offer their portion of gold to the daughters, and the king invites everyone to Peter's funeral "orgies." The misuse of "obsequies" confirms the suspicions of the local doctor, who laughs as he realizes the two are frauds. When the doctor tries to convince the daughters to reject the duke and the king, the daughters give the money back to prove their faith in their "uncles."

The next morning, Joanna quizzes Huck about England, the king, and church. Similar to his disguise as "Sarah Mary Williams," Huck becomes confused trying to keep up with his lies, and the trust and kindness of the daughters makes him realize that he has to act. Later that evening, Huck discovers where the duke and the king hid the gold. He takes the $6,000 and waits for the opportunity to restore it to the rightful owners.

Commentary

The king's "tears and flapdoodle" speech is a hilarious example of a con man at work, preying on the faith and the perceptions of conventional grief of his victims. Despite the obvious fraud recognized by readers, the family and the town easily accept the king and the duke as English. Huck is appalled by the act, but he also recognizes the persuasive power of "soul-butter" (flattery) and its effect on the ignorant townspeople. The humor increases when the king confuses "orgies" with funeral "obsequies," and his explanation of the Greek and Hebrew origins of the word only adds to the ridiculousness of the scene. In a sense, Twain is commenting on humankind's capacity for ignorance, for everyone except the doctor falls victim to the scam.

After viewing the king's speech, Huck realizes how clever, and thus how dangerous, the duke and the king actually are. To act against them clearly jeopardizes his own well being, but, more important, it also jeopardizes the chances of freedom for Jim. Despite the danger, Huck concludes he must return the gold to the daughters.

Glossary

doxolojer the doxology; a hymn of praise to God.

soul-butter flattery.

yaller-boys gold coins.

obsequies funeral rites or ceremonies.

Congress-water mineral water from Saratoga said to have medicinal properities.

Chapters 27 and 28

Summary

The same evening, Huck sneaks downstairs to try and hide the bag of gold. The front door is locked, however, and when Huck hears Mary Jane coming, he is forced to hide the gold in Peter Wilks' coffin. Because so many people are in the house, Huck does not have the opportunity to retrieve the money.

The funeral proceeds, and Huck realizes he does not know whether the gold is still in the coffin or if someone else has discovered it. After the funeral, the king announces that the estate will be sold in two days. The daughters appear to accept the sale until the king breaks up a slave family and sells them to different traders.

Mary Jane cannot bear to think of the separated family and the mother and the children never seeing one another again. Because he wants to comfort her, Huck blurts out that the slave family will see each other in the next two weeks. When Mary Jane promises to leave the house if Huck will tell her how he knows this, Huck tells the entire story of the king and the duke and how they have fooled everyone.

Mary Jane wants to tar and feather the con men immediately, but Huck reminds her of her promise and explains that "I'd be all right; but there'd be another person that you don't know about who'd be in big trouble." She honors her promise, and Huck gives her a note that explains where the missing gold can be found. The other daughters are confused about Mary Jane's absence, and the confusion grows when two more men arrive claiming to be Harvey and William.

Commentary

Style & Language

In Chapter 27, Twain extends his satire to the pomp and circumstance surrounding the funeral service of Peter Wilks. The dark humor of the funeral scene is evident with the actions of the undertaker and the comical interlude of the dog and the rat. When the service is interrupted by the noise of the dog, the undertaker solves the disturbance and then proceeds to tell the mourners that "*He had a rat!*" Huck's following comment that "there warn't no more popular man in town than what that undertaker was" is yet another satiric barb directed at the subject of death.

In contrast to the burlesque humor of the funeral and its concerned mourners, Chapter 28 serves to establish Mary Jane's sense of compassion, an important example for Huck to follow. In witnessing her reaction to the plight of the slave family, Huck learns another valuable lesson about the humanity of slaves and their close familial bonds. The scene provokes memories of Jim's own claim that he will steal his children out of slavery in order to preserve his family. More important, the scene forces Huck to act based on both his instincts and his conscience. Not only will he tell the daughters where to find the gold, he will also tell them of the entire scam so that the slave family will not be separated.

Huck's decision to help the daughters should not be overlooked. To this point, Huck has generally aligned himself with tricksters and con men; he displays, after all, all of the huckster qualities that the duke and the king use. When the duke and king dupe the people of Bricksville, Huck feels no remorse because the town is morally void and generally squalid. When the duke and the king con the Wilks daughters, however, Huck is outraged and realizes he must intervene, regardless of the consequences.

One of the more powerful human statements is the act of sacrifice, and Huck's resolve to help the daughters illustrates the change that has come over his character. His decision to act foreshadows the novel's climatic moment in Chapter 31.

Glossary

smouch steal.

melodeum melodeon; a small keyboard organ.

erysipelas an acute infectious disease of the skin or mucous membranes caused by a streptococcus and characterized by local inflammation and fever.

consumption tuberculosis.

harrow a frame with spikes or sharp-edged disks, drawn by a horse or tractor and used for breaking up and leveling plowed ground, covering seeds, rooting up weeds, etc.

muggins a fool.

Chapters 29 and 30

Summary

Even Huck recognizes that the new claimants to Peter Wilks' fortune appear to be English compared to the duke and the king. The older gentleman introduces himself as Harvey and says they can prove their identity when they retrieve their baggage. In response, the king laughs and tells the crowd it is not surprising that the new "brothers" cannot immediately prove their claim. At this point, the crowd still believes the duke and the king are the true brothers, but the doctor convinces everyone that they must investigate further. After questioning Huck about his English heritage, the town lawyer, Levi Bell, tells Huck that he obviously is not used to lying.

The older gentleman says he can prove who he is because he knows what is tattooed on Peter Wilks' chest. The king says it is a small blue arrow, and the older gentleman says it is a dim "P" and "B." The lawyer decides the only one way to be positive is to exhume Peter Wilks and have a look at his chest.

When they open the coffin, they discover the bag of gold on the body's chest. The crowd becomes so excited that Huck is able to slip away, and he and Jim escape on the raft. Before they can get very far, however, they see the king and duke have also escaped. Jim and Huck realize they are not free from the con men. The duke and the king blame one another for stealing the bag of gold, but after getting drunk, they again become comrades and start working their schemes on new villages.

Commentary

The introduction of the new Harvey and William adds another element of hilarity to the con men's inheritance scam. The contrast between the two sets of "brothers" is obvious, and the ensuing investigation underscores both the ignorance of the town and the eagerness of the townspeople to witness a dispute. Instead of reacting with anger, the town enjoys the added confusion and as the questions continue, the humor and suspense build.

Literary Device

Huck's role as a servant is called into question, and unlike previous escapades, Huck is unable to convince the doctor and lawyer of his English ancestry. Instead of accepting Huck's story, the lawyer tells Huck, "I wouldn't strain myself if I was you. I reckon you ain't used to lying . . . You do it pretty awkward." Although Huck's entire journey has been based on lies and deception, he is unable to fool intelligent men for even a moment. The irony is apparent, as is Huck's reluctance to try and adapt his story. Instead of attempting to lie his way out of another predicament, Huck chooses to remain quiet and observe the comical investigation.

The con men's unwillingness to leave without selling all of the family's possessions represents the greed of the two men. Ironically, it is this same type of greed that allows Huck and the duke and the king to escape. When the townsmen see the gold in Peter Wilks' coffin, they are unable to resist and the ensuing melee is reminiscent of Bricksville. Twain's commentary on the greed and ignorance of the mob mentality is solidified with the duke and the king's escape.

Glossary

cravats neckerchiefs or scarves.

shekel a half-ounce gold or silver coin of the ancient Hebrews.

gabble to talk rapidly and incoherently; jabber; chatter.

Chapter 31

Summary

With the temperature rising and the landscape scattered with Spanish moss, Huck realizes that they are a long way from home. The new schemes of the duke and the king barely bring in enough money for liquor, so the two men begin to plot and whisper about their next scam. Huck and Jim are concerned about the clandestine behavior of the con men, and when Huck finally sees a chance to escape, he discovers that the duke and the king have made a fake handbill and turned in Jim for a $40 reward.

Huck is furious with the con men because "after all we'd done for them scoundrels . . . they could have the heart to serve Jim and make him a slave again all his life." As Huck ponders his choices, his conscience begins to trouble him again. He cannot help but feel guilty for assisting Jim, despite the fact that his instincts constantly force him into that role. After trying to pray for resolution, Huck writes a letter to Miss Watson detailing where Jim is and signs it "Huck Finn." After he finishes the letter, he feels momentary relief and is confident that he has saved himself from going to hell for helping a slave.

Instead of being satisfied with his decision, however, Huck begins to replay their trip down the river. He reminisces about the two of them "a-floating along, talking and singing and laughing" and cannot force himself to see Jim as someone disgraceful. Huck trembles as he again picks up Miss Watson's letter and realizes that the struggle must stop: He must decide forever between two things: heaven and hell. He pauses for a minute, then declares "All right, then, I'll go to hell" and tears the letter to pieces. Once Huck makes his decision to betray society for Jim, he immediately plots to steal Jim back out of slavery.

Commentary

If Chapter 18 is the end of the first segment of the novel, Chapter 31 is the end of the second segment and one of the most important chapters in *Adventures of Huckleberry Finn*. Up until this point, the novel has wavered back and forth between the river and the shore, with humorous and cruel events constantly bombarding the reader. The conflicts of individual versus society, freedom versus civilization, and sentimentalism versus realism, as well as Huck's struggle between right and wrong, are all revealed in Huck and Jim's journey. And all come to a head in Huck's eventual decision. In the midst of these events rests Huck's inner struggle to ignore his conscience and transcend his environment.

The catalyst for Huck's action is the sale of Jim back into slavery. Ironically, Huck believes he will be shunned by his community and doom himself to literal hell if he aids Jim. Despite this realization, Huck's proclamation "All right, then, I'll *go* to hell," ends his struggle in a concise and powerful moment, which is the climax of the novel.

Theme

In light of his climatic decision, Huck's entire narrative symbolizes a search for his own conscience and identity, and this identity is shaped by his attempt to make moral evaluations despite the pressures of surrounding theological and societal codes. That Huck has not been able to reconcile his struggle should not come as a surprise to readers, for Huck's sacrifice is lost on the racist society that pervaded nineteenth-century America. The statement becomes even more powerful when readers realize that Huck's decision to recognize Jim's humanity is not shared by the rest of society.

Character Insight

Above all, it is important to note that Huck's declaration, despite the surrounding satire and bitter irony, elevates him to a heroic character. Twain, however, cannot help but infuse more subtle irony even after Huck's decision, and Huck's reasoning that "as long as I was in [hell], and in for good, I might as well go the whole hog" notifies readers that the novel will take yet another turn in its last segment.

Glossary

Spanish Moss a plant often found growing in long, graceful strands from the branches of trees in the south eastern U.S.

doggery a saloon.

Chapters 32 and 33

Summary

After learning of Jim's location, Huck arrives at the Phelps farm. He surmises the Phelps' "little one-horse cotton plantation," but before he can reach the door, he is surrounded by all sorts of barking dogs. After a slave woman runs them off, another woman comes out of the house and says, "It's *you,* at last!—*ain't* it?" as if she is expecting Huck. Before Huck realizes what he is doing, he answers yes and the woman grabs him and hugs him like she has known him all of her life.

The woman, who Huck learns is named "Aunt Sally," asks him about his trip and then asks him about the family. Huck realizes he is in a bind, but just before Huck confesses, the husband arrives and Aunt Sally introduces Huck as none other than Tom Sawyer. Huck is stunned momentarily and then realizes that he has somehow managed to stumble upon Tom's relatives. After answering several questions about the Sawyer family, Huck heads back to the river in hopes of finding the real Tom who must be on his way.

When Huck gets halfway to town, he finds Tom Sawyer. At first, Tom thinks Huck is a ghost. After Huck explains the situation with Jim, Tom declares that he will "*help* you steal him" out of slavery.

When they arrive at the Phelps farm, Tom makes up an elaborate story and introduces himself as Tom's brother, Sid Sawyer. Huck and Tom learn that the king and the duke are in town to perform and that Jim has warned the townspeople that the upcoming show is a fraud. Huck and Tom sneak out to try and tell the duke and the king, but they soon come upon the chaotic mob who has already tarred and feathered the con men.

Commentary

Literary
Device

Chapter 32 begins what could be called the last segment of the novel. Huck's solemn narration is evident at the beginning of the chapter, when he describes the breeze that occasionally washes over the farm. For Huck, the breeze comes across as a whisper of spirits long dead, and readers are reminded of those that have already died earlier in the novel. The entire journey appears to weigh heavily on Huck, and at one point he "wished I was dead" after hearing the lonesome hum of a spinning wheel. In a sense, the Phelps farm is symbolic of Huck's return back to civilization. Although he and Jim have traveled hundreds of miles down the Mississippi River, they find themselves in a situation very similar to the life they left with Miss Watson and the Widow Douglas.

Huck's climatic decision to free Jim has brought about an unconscious epiphany or revelation in Huck's character, and when he nears the farmhouse, he does not pause, but looks to "Providence to put the right words in my mouth." Although Huck has always been prone to improvisation, he now credits his ability to Providence. The statement reveals that Huck, despite his own belief that he is now damned, places his fate (and Jim's) in the hands of another. Ironically, the person who arrives is the real Tom Sawyer, the nephew of Silas and Sally Phelps.

Literary critics have argued that the coincidence of Huck arriving at the Phelps farm is implausible in a "realistic" novel. It is important to remember, however, that Twain's original intentions for the novel included Tom as a main character. The first edition was entitled *Adventures of Huckleberry Finn (Tom Sawyer's Comrade)*, and therefore it is not surprising that Tom reenters the novel before its conclusion.

Tom's arrival on the Phelps farm signals that a new leader will control the future of Huck and Jim. Whereas Huck and Jim shared responsibility for their fate, Tom now dictates their plans of "adventure" and escape. By allowing Tom to control the conclusion of the novel, *Huckleberry Finn* turns away from Huck's constant struggle with his conscience and reverts back to a story intended for boys and girls. The dramatic tonal shift can be attributed to several factors, including the fact that *Huckleberry Finn* was written in three stages. But it also reflects Twain's indecision over the conclusion of the novel and how to reconcile his scathing social commentary on American, and especially Southern, society.

Tom's reintroduction signals that playful and harmless pranks are soon to follow. The reunion of the two boys, however, does not completely overshadow the violent setting that Twain has carefully constructed. Huck still observes the squalid nature of "civilization" and tries to compensate through kindness, a trait reminiscent of the Widow

Douglas. The tarring and feathering of the duke and the king reveals Huck's sympathetic view toward everyone, even those who have been cruel to him. Instead of standing by and watching the two con men receive their punishment, Huck tries to save the duke and the king from the town and a fate that could include death. When he fails to save the duke and the king, he comments that "Human beings can be awful cruel to one another." The statement could be applied to the entire novel, as Huck has witnessed countless incidents that were void of humanity.

Glossary

smokehouse a building, especially an outbuilding on a farm, where meats, fish, etc. are smoked in order to cure and flavor them.

bars a thing that blocks the way or prevents entrance or further movement, as in a sandbar.

Methusalem Methuselah, one of the biblical patriarchs who was said to live 969 years.

Chapters 34 and 35

Summary

Tom discovers that Jim is being held in a small farm cabin, and the two boys discuss plans to free Jim from captivity. Huck's logical plan is to steal the keys from Uncle Silas, quickly unlock Jim, and immediately leave on the raft. Tom argues that the plan is too simple and as "mild as goosemilk." After they examine the cabin where Jim is being held, Huck suggests that they tear off one board for Jim to escape. Tom again argues that the plan is not complicated enough and then decides that they should dig Jim out because doing so will take a couple of weeks. When a slave brings food to Jim, the boys go along and whisper to Jim that they are going to set him free.

Tom and Huck begin making plans for an elaborate escape, and each step becomes more complicated and time-consuming. Tom argues that Jim will need a rope ladder and other items such as case-knives and a journal, because the escape must be done just like the prison novels he has read.

Commentary

The opportunity to burlesque Tom's romanticism and infuse humor back into the novel comes at the price of Jim's perceived freedom. In actuality, Jim has already been set free by the late Miss Watson's will, and readers will learn this startling fact at the end of the novel. However, because both Huck and Jim are unaware of Jim's freedom, they agree to follow Tom's extravagant plans for a dramatic escape.

The elaborate escape plan provides Tom the opportunity to call upon several of the prison stories and adventure novels he has read. By combining unnecessary tactics such as a tunnel and devices such as a rope ladder, the entire plan becomes a comical romantic farce. The incongruity of Huck's logic in the face of Tom's imagination creates several humorous exchanges, and the farce is reminiscent of Twain's earlier work with *Tom Sawyer*. For example, when Tom says that Jim needs to keep a journal, Huck replies, "Journal your granny—*Jim* can't write."

Huck's practical response is both humorous and revealing at the same time. On the surface, it is obvious that Jim does not need to keep a journal, but the fact that Jim is captive during this time is an overriding shadow on the slapstick humor. The ability to read and write was not common among anyone in the mid-1800s, and because Jim is a slave, his being able to write is much more unlikely. More important, however, is the realization that Huck cannot stop the nonsensical plans because he and Jim are trapped within the confines of a racist society.

Theme

Neither Huck nor Jim is able to dissuade or alter Tom's plans except in minor ways, and their failed attempts symbolize their ill-fated efforts to truly escape civilization's conventions. The biting satire is obvious when Huck wonders about the logic of digging a tunnel with ordinary case-knives. When he questions Tom, Tom replies that "It don't make no difference how foolish it is, it's the *right* way . . . .. And there ain't no *other way*, that ever *I* heard of, and I've read all the books that gives any information about these things." As a representative of proper society, Tom summarizes civilization's reliance on tradition and existing laws that have been recorded, despite their lack of humanity and compassion.

Glossary

fox-fire the luminescence of decaying wood and plant remains, caused by various fungi.

seneskal seneschal, a steward or major-domo in the household of a medieval noble.

Langudoc Languedoc, historical region of southern France.

Navarre historical region and former kingdom in northeast Spain and southwest France.

Chapters 36, 37, and 38

Summary

The next evening, Tom and Huck try to use the case-knives to dig a tunnel under the cabin, but after a few hours, they realize they need better tools. Tom decides they will use pick-axes and shovels and pretend that they are case-knives. The next night, Tom and Huck easily dig into Jim's cabin and wake him. Jim listens to Tom's plans and agrees to go along with them even though he thinks they do not make sense. Tom assures Jim that they will change the plans immediately if something goes wrong.

The boys begin smuggling "escape" tools into the cabin, and Aunt Sally notices that items are missing from the house. To confuse her, Tom and Huck continually take and replace sheets and spoons until Aunt Sally does not know how many she had to start with. Finally they tear up one of the sheets and smuggle it into Jim's cabin along with some tins plates. Following Tom's instructions on how to write mysterious messages, Jim marks on the tin plates and then throws them out the window.

The next day, Tom continues to find new distractions for Jim's escape. Tom writes down some inscriptions for Jim to carve into the wall but then realizes the walls are wooden. To be done properly and according to the books, Tom says they must have stone. The boys try to roll a large grindstone into the cabin but are not strong enough. Jim climbs out of the cabin and helps them roll the stone the rest of the way. Despite Jim's protests, Tom decides that the cabin needs other residents, including spiders and snakes, in order to make it a proper dungeon and Jim a proper prisoner.

Commentary

In Chapters 36 through 38, the novel slips further into the farce as neither Huck nor Jim understand why they must perform all of these ludicrous acts before Jim can escape. Ironically, Huck and Jim view Tom as a representative of society and education, and because of this, they feel that Tom must know the best way for them to escape.

Theme

Jim's continued enslavement is both absurd and grotesque and is a harsh comment on the racial condition of post-Civil War America. As mentioned earlier, Miss Watson has already set Jim free in her will, but the ability to transcend and change society's perception is not as easily accomplished. Jim, therefore, remains captive to others despite the fact that he has, indeed, been freed.

It is important to remember that *Huck Finn* was written in the 20 years following the Civil War, and the entire novel reflects Twain's own post-Civil War observations. Although the Union made some attempt at Southern reconstruction, the South quickly fell into a squalid and segregated ruin. Conditions for newly freed slaves were no doubt improved, but the longed-for freedom had not come with changed perceptions, acceptance, or equality.

Glossary

dog-fennel any of several weeds or wildflowers of the composite family, having daisylike flower heads.

scutcheon escutcheon a shield or shield-shaped surface on which a coat of arms is displayed.

juice harp jew's harp, a small musical instrument consisting of a lyre-shaped metal frame held between the teeth and played by plucking a projecting bent piece with the finger.

mullen stalks stalks of the mullein, a tall plant of the figwort family, with spikes of yellow, lavender, or white flowers.

Chapters 39 and 40

Summary

Tom and Huck capture several rats to put in Jim's cabin, but one of the Phelps boys finds the box and lets all of the rats free into the house. After several creatures are accidentally freed in the Phelps' house, Tom and Huck finally capture enough rats, spiders, and snakes, and put them in Jim's cabin. Jim complains that there is not enough room for him, and if he ever becomes free he "wouldn't ever be a prisoner again, not for a salary."

After three weeks, everything is finally ready for the grand escape. To finish off the scheme, Tom writes an anonymous letter to the Phelps saying that a "desperate gang of cutthroats" will attempt to steal Jim out of the cabin.

Huck returns to the house to pick up some butter and finds that the Phelps have gathered 15 men to battle the gang of cutthroats. Alarmed, Huck sneaks out the window and warns Tom that the men are here, and they must all escape immediately. When the men come to the cabin, Jim and the boys slip out of the hole and head for the river amidst shouts and gunshots. They make it to the raft but then discover that Tom has been shot in the calf. Tom tells them to shove off, but Jim will not leave until a doctor has looked at Tom.

Commentary

The entire Phelps' household is in complete disarray when the escape actually begins. In this manner, the novel has moved even further from the peaceful tranquility of the raft and the river to the chaos of society and the shore. Symbolizing the clash between Romanticism and Realism, Huck and Tom continue to display juxtaposing approaches to the escape and the situation. The arrival of a town posse frightens Huck, but Tom is delighted. When Huck tells Tom that the house is full of men with guns, Tom replies, "*Ain't* it bully!" as if the entire escape is a dramatic work of fiction.

Although readers have already recognized Jim as compassionate and caring, Chapter 40 reinforces Jim's qualities of bravery and loyalty. When they discover that Tom has been shot, Jim adamantly refuses to leave and says, "I doan' budge a step out'n dis place @'dout a *doctor*; not if it's forty year!" The statement reinforces Jim as a heroic figure capable of sacrifice.

Glossary

allycumpain elecampane, a tall, hairy perennial plant of the composite family, having flower heads with many slender, yellow rays.

Chapters 41 and 42

Summary

Huck quickly locates a doctor and tells him that his brother "had a dream . . . and it shot him." The doctor heads for the raft but will not let Huck come along because the canoe is too small. Exhausted, Huck falls asleep until the next morning. When he wakes up, he runs into Uncle Silas, and the two of them go back to the Phelps farm, which is full of local men discussing the strange cabin and its contents. The farmers decide that Jim must have been helped by several slaves and the writing is some sort of "secret African" language.

The next day, Tom and Jim arrive at the Phelps' with the doctor and several of the farmers. Tom is on a mattress and Jim has his hands tied. The men argue whether or not to hang Jim, and the doctor explains how Jim helped with Tom instead of running away.

The next morning Tom wakes up and begins to tell Aunt Sally how he and "Tom" (Huck) orchestrated the entire escape. Tom relishes the retelling until he hears that Jim is still in captivity. Tom rises up in bed and demands that they free Jim because he has known all along that Miss Watson had died and set Jim free in her will. At that moment, Aunt Polly arrives, and Tom and Huck are forced to reveal their true identities.

Commentary

With Tom unable to direct the plans, Huck again takes control of the story and makes decisions based on his common sense and logic. Instead of listening to Tom's intricate plan to fetch a doctor, Huck trusts his own ability to tell lies and control the situation. Although the doctor is somewhat suspicious of Huck's story, when Huck returns to the farm, he finds that the entire community has been drawn into Tom's fanciful escape. The ignorance and gullibility of the farmers is easily seen as they try to reconstruct and understand the escape.

Jim's refusal to leave Tom in Chapter 40 becomes more significant in Chapter 42 when he allows himself to be recaptured. As with Huck's earlier decision to sacrifice his soul to free Jim, Jim sacrifices his freedom and, quite possibly, his life by staying with Tom. Because Jim is thought to be a runaway slave, the local men "was very huffy, and some of them wanted to hang Jim as an example." Jim is, no doubt, fully aware that if he is recaptured he might be lynched, and this realization gives more credence to his role as a heroic figure at the end of the novel. The doctor who saves Tom also lauds Jim's character, and this praise further establishes his position.

As mentioned earlier, one of the most controversial elements of the novel is the fact that Jim is already free during the escape. When Tom realizes that Jim has been recaptured, he sits up in bed and declares that "They hain't no *right* to shut him up! *Shove!*—and don't you lose a minute. Turn him loose! he ain't no slave; he's as free as any cretur that walks this earth!" The realization stuns both the characters of the novel and the readers, as it becomes clear that the entire escape was unnecessary.

The turn of events serves two purposes. On the surface, the realization finalizes the separate attitudes and beliefs of Tom and Huck. Tom's Romanticism is now viewed as harmful instead of playful, and his connection with society illustrates its overarching lack of compassion toward the plight of slaves in nineteenth-century America. Beneath the surface, however, is the subtle message that no one, regardless of race or social standing or location, is free from civilization and its misconceptions. Tom's statement, then, is one of Twain's harshest and most ironic comments on the American condition.

Glossary

Nebokoodneezer Nebuchadnezzar, king of Babylonia who conquered Jerusalem, destroyed the Temple, and deported many Jews into Babylonia (586 BC).

Chapter The Last

Summary

Huck asks Tom what they would have done if the escape had worked, and Tom says they would have continued having adventures down to the end of the Mississippi. After they finished, they could ride back home on a steamship, in style, and they would all be heroes.

In conclusion, Huck tells readers that Tom is well now and wears his bullet around his neck on a watch-guard. He says that, if he had known how much trouble it was to write a book, he would not have tried it. Now that he is finished, he must "light out for the Territory ahead of the rest" in order to stay one step ahead of civilization and live in true freedom. Aunt Sally now wants to adopt Huck officially and "sivilize" him, but Huck says he " . . . can't stand it. I been there before."

Commentary

Although Huck and Jim have both undergone changes in character, the novel returns to its beginnings at the conclusion with the Widow Douglas trying to "sivilize" Huck. The last chapter allows Twain to comment on the process of writing and the difficulty of completing *Adventures of Huckleberry Finn.* Twain's difficulty was due, in large part, to his struggle to decide between a social commentary and a children's adventure novel. Although Huck declares that if "I'd 'a' knowed what a trouble it was to make a book I wouldn't 'a' tackled it," the suggestion is that there will be yet another adventure for Huck, and yet another novel for Twain. Always the maverick, Huck announces that he will continue to try and avoid the trappings of civilization and seek his own freedom.

CHARACTER ANALYSES

Huckleberry Finn

When determining who should narrate the novel, Twain first considered the popular character, Tom Sawyer. Tom, after all, had garnered an enormous following from his own tale, *The Adventures of Tom Sawyer*. But Twain felt that Tom's romantic personality would not be right for the novel, and so he chose Tom's counterpart, Huckleberry Finn. Huck is the most important figure in *Huck Finn*. It is his literal, pragmatic approach to his surroundings and his inner struggle with his conscience that make him one of the most important and recognizable figures in American literature.

As a coming of age character in the late nineteenth century, Huck views his surroundings with a practical and logical lens. His observations are not filled with judgments; instead, Huck observes his environment and gives realistic descriptions of the Mississippi River and the culture that dominates the towns that dot its shoreline from Missouri south.

Huck's practical and often socially naive views and perceptions provide much of the satirical humor of the novel. It is important to note, however, that Huck himself never laughs at the incongruities he describes. For example, Huck simply accepts, at face value, the abstract social and religious tenets pressed upon him by Miss Watson until his experiences cause him to make decisions in which his learned values and his natural feelings come in conflict. When Huck is unable to conform to the rules, he accepts that it is his own deficiency, not the rule, that is bad. Abstractly, he does not recognize the contradiction of "loving thy neighbor" and enforcing slavery at the same time. He observes the racist and anti-government rants of his ignorant father but does not condemn him because it is the "accepted" view in his world. Huck simply reports what he sees, and the deadpan narration allows Twain to depict a realistic view of common ignorance, slavery, and the inhumanity that follows.

As with several of the frontier literary characters that came before him, Huck possesses the ability to adapt to almost any situation through deceit. He is playful but practical, inventive but logical, compassionate but realistic, and these traits allow him to survive the abuse of Pap, the violence of a feud, and the wiles of river con men. To persevere in these situations, Huck lies, cheats, steals, and defrauds his way down the river. These traits are part of the reason that *Huck Finn* was viewed as a book not acceptable for children, yet they are also traits that allow Huck to survive his surroundings and, in the conclusion, make the right decision.

Because Huck believes that the laws of society are just, he condemns himself as a traitor and a villain for acting against them and aiding Jim. More important, Huck believes that he will lose his chance at Providence by helping a slave. When Huck declares, "All right, then, I'll *go* to hell," he refuses his place in society and heaven, and the magnitude of his decision is what solidifies his role as a heroic figure.

Jim

Along with Huck, Jim is the other major character in the novel and one of the most controversial figures in American literature. There are several possibilities in terms of the inspiration for Jim. Twain's autobiography speaks of Uncle Daniel, who was a slave at his Uncle John Quarles farm. Twain described Uncle Daniel as a man who was well known for his sympathy toward others and his honest heart. Another possible inspiration for Jim came from Twain's relationship with John Lewis, a tenant farmer at Quarry farm. In a letter to William Dean Howells, Twain recalled how Lewis had once saved his entire family when a horse-drawn carriage broke away on the farm. Lewis had corralled the horse and forever earned the respect of Twain, who also praised Lewis' work ethic and attitude. Several critics have also suggested that Jim was modeled after Twain's butler, George Griffin, who was a part of Twain's staff during the years that he was writing *Huck Finn*.

In the beginning of the novel, Jim is depicted as simple and trusting, to the point of gullibility. These qualities are not altered during the course of the novel; instead, they are fleshed out and prove to be positives instead of negatives. Jim's simple nature becomes common sense, and he constantly chooses the right path for him and Huck to follow. For example, when Huck and Jim are on Jackson's Island, Jim observes the nervous actions of birds and predicts that it will rain. Jim's prediction comes true as a huge storm comes upon the island. The moment is an important one, for it establishes Jim as an authority figure and readers recognize his experience and intelligence. Jim's insight is also revealed when he recognizes the duke and the king to be frauds. Like Huck, Jim realizes he cannot stop the con men from controlling the raft, but he tells Huck that "I doan' hanker for no mo' un um, Huck. Dese is all I kin stan'."

Jim's most important quality, however, is his "gullible" nature. As the novel progresses, this nature reveals itself as complete faith and trust in his friends, especially Huck. The one trait that does not fluctuate throughout the novel is Jim's belief in Huck. After Huck makes up a story to preserve Jim's freedom in Chapter 16, Jim remarks that he will never forget Huck's kindness. Jim's love for Huck, however, extends past their friendship to the relationship of parent and child. When Huck and Jim come upon the dead man on the floating house, Jim warns Huck not to look at the man's face. The gesture is kind, but when readers learn later that the man was Pap Finn, they realize the affection Jim has for Huck. Jim does not want Huck to suffer through the pain of seeing his dead father, and this moment establishes Jim as a father figure to Huck.

Jim's actions, no doubt, are partly a result of his inability to distance himself from the society in which he has been conditioned. His existence has been permeated by social and legal laws that require him to place another race above his own, regardless of the consequences. But as with Huck, Jim is willing to sacrifice his life for his friends. There are countless opportunities for Jim to leave Huck during the tale, yet he remains by Huck's side so the two of them can escape together. When Huck and Jim become separated in the fog, Jim tells Huck that his "heart wuz mos' broke bekase you wuz los', en I didn' k'yer no mo' what bcome er me en de raf'." Jim's freedom, then, is not worth the price of Huck's life, and readers are constantly reminded that Jim would readily risk his own life to aid Huck. When Huck is taken in by the Shepherdsons, Jim waits in the swamp and devises a plan where both of them can continue down the river. Moreover, when Jim has the chance to be free at the end of the novel, he stays by Tom Sawyer's side, another example of his loyalty. Jim's logic, compassion, intelligence, and above all, his loyalty toward Huck, Tom, and his own family, establish him as a heroic figure.

Tom Sawyer

If Huck is the consummate realist of the novel, Tom Sawyer is the representative romantic. When readers are first introduced to Tom, they immediately recognize his role as a leader, or controlling agent, of the situation. The gang is labeled "Tom Sawyer's Gang" because he is the one that controls the activities and pursuits. These activities, however, are always based upon Tom's exaggerated notions of adventure. Basing his experience on the fanciful books he has read, Tom tries to adapt his life and the life of others to that which he has read. The end result is a burlesque of sensibility and emotion, two literary agents that Twain despised.

Tom's role as a romantic is extremely important because of its juxtaposition with Huck's literal approach. Although Tom declares that his gang will pursue the exploits of piracy and murder, in reality the gang succeeds in "charging down on hog-drovers and women in carts taking garden stuff to the market." The vision of the young boys disrupting women bound for the market provides much of the harmless humor during the early pages of *Huck Finn,* and Tom is largely responsible for the slapstick approach. Tom's constant barrage of exaggeration, however, contrasts with Huck's deadpan narration, and Huck can "see no profit" in Tom's methods. Where Huck is practical, Tom is emotional; where Huck is logical, Tom is extravagant. Despite the fact that readers easily recognize Tom's ideas as folly, Huck does not question Tom's authority. On the contrary, Huck believes that Tom's knowledge is above his own, and this includes Tom's attitude toward slavery.

In a sense, Tom represents the civilized society that Huck and Jim leave behind on their flight down the river. When Tom reappears with his fancied notions of escape from the Phelps farm, Jim again becomes a gullible slave and Huck becomes a simple agent to Tom. There is no doubt that Tom is intelligent, and he does state that they will free Jim immediately if there is trouble, but the ensuing ruse suggests that Tom is unable to shake society and the Romantic idealism he possesses, even when Jim's freedom is at stake.

CRITICAL ESSAYS

Theme—Freedom versus Civilization

As with most works of literature, *Adventures of Huckleberry Finn* incorporates several themes developed around a central plot create a story. In this case, the story is of a young boy, Huck, and an escaped slave, Jim, and their moral, ethical, and human development during an odyssey down the Mississippi River that brings them into many conflicts with greater society. What Huck and Jim seek is freedom, and this freedom is sharply contrasted with the existing civilization along the great river. The practice of combining contrasting themes is common throughout *Huck Finn*, and Twain uses the resulting contradictions for the purposes of humor and insight. If freedom versus civilization is the overarching theme of the novel, it is illustrated through several thematic contradictions, including Tom's Romanticism versus Huck's Realism.

The Romantic literary movement began in the late eighteenth century and prospered into the nineteenth century. Described as a revolt against the rationalism that had defined the Neo-Classical movement (dominate during the seventeenth and early eighteenth century), Romanticism placed heavy emphasis on imagination, emotion, and sensibility. Heroic feats, dangerous adventures, and inflated prose marked the resulting literature, which exalted the senses and emotion over intellect and reason. Authors such as Harriet Beecher Stowe, Nathaniel Hawthorne, and Edgar Allan Poe all enjoyed immense popularity. In addition, the writers of the New England Renaissance—Emerson, Longfellow, Holmes, and Whittier—dominated literary study, and the public's appetite for extravagance appeared to be insatiable.

By the end of the 1870s, however, the great age of Romanticism appeared to be reaching its zenith. Bawdy humor and a realistic portrayal of the new American frontier were quickly displacing the refined culture of the New England literary circle. William Dean Howells described the new movement as "nothing more and nothing less than the truthful treatment of material." A new brand of literature emerged from the ashes of refined Romanticism, and this literature attacked existing icons, both literary and societal. The attack was not surprising, for the new authors, such as Mark Twain, had risen from middle-class values, and thus they were in direct contrast to the educated and genteel writers who had come before them. Literary Realism strove to depict an America as it really was, unfettered by Romanticism and often cruel and harsh in its reality. In *Huck Finn,* this contrast reveals itself in the guise of Tom and Huck.

Representing the Romantic movement, Tom gleefully pulls the logical Huck into his schemes and adventures. When the boys come together at the beginning of the novel to create a band of robbers, Tom tells the gang that if anyone whispers their secrets, the boy and his entire family will be killed. The exaggerated purpose of the gang is comical in itself; however, when the gang succeeds in terrorizing a Sunday-school picnic, Twain succeeds in his burlesque of Romanticism. The more Tom tries to convince Huck and the rest of the boys that they are stealing jewelry from Arabs and Spaniards, the more ridiculous the scene becomes. After the gang steals turnips and Tom labels them as jewelry, Huck finally decides to resign because he "couldn't see no profit in it."

Because the practical Huck is an agent of Realism, he finally decides that the "adventures" are simply lies of Tom Sawyer. Huck cannot see the purpose behind Tom's reasoning and imagination, and his literal approach to Tom's extravagance provides much of the novel's humor.

Although Tom resurfaces at the novel's conclusion, Twain makes use of other devices to attack Romanticism during the course of the novel. When Huck hears a "twig snap" in Chapter 1, the subtle allusion is to James Fenimore Cooper and his Leatherstocking Tales, such as *The Last of the Mohicans*. In "Fenimore Cooper's Literary Offenses," a satire of the early-nineteenth-century American novelist, Twain argued against the Romanticism that caused Cooper to prize "his broken twig above all the rest of his effects . . .. In fact, the Leatherstocking Series ought to have been called the Broken Twig series." In addition, when Huck and Jim come upon a crippled steamboat during their flight down the river, it is not coincidental that the boat's name is the *Walter Scott,* the same name as the Romantic author of *Ivanhoe* and *The Abbott.*

Twain's burlesque of Romanticism represents more, however, than simply a literary method of humor. The imagination of Tom also symbolizes the constructed idealism of civilization, and its contrast with Jim's right to freedom becomes evident at the end of the novel. In this manner, the mistaken belief that nineteenth-century American society, especially in the South, had overcome its racial bigotry and hatred is as ludicrous as Tom's extravagant plan to free Jim from the Phelps farm.

In contrast, as Huck questions the validity of Tom's Romanticism, he also questions the validity of the society around him, including its religious teachings and social laws. But, because Huck believes that Tom's education and upbringing make his judgment sound, Huck feels that he is the one who is destined for hell. The satiric comment is a harsh one and notifies readers that the interplay between Tom and Huck is not simply for humor. The contrast between Tom's Romanticism and Huck's Realism is also Twain's condemnation of a society that was still divided and unequal even after the Emancipation Proclamation.

Characterization—Pap versus Jim

There is no doubt that one of the most important literary elements in a work is characterization: The creation of a group of personalities who function as representatives of a fictional world are as vital to a novel's story as its many themes. For Mark Twain, the challenge was to embody fictional characters with realistic traits and personalities; that is, his characters had to be as believable and as recognizable as the people readers confronted every day. To accomplish this feat, Twain frequently called upon his childhood experiences to create some of the most memorable characters in American literature.

The expanse of characters that blanket the pages of *Huck Finn* are numerous. Certainly Huck is an incredible character study, with his literal and pragmatic approach to his surroundings and his constant battle with his conscience.

Huck's companion, Jim, is yet another character worthy of analysis. At a period in American history when most African-American characters were depicted as fools or "Uncle Tom's," Jim's triumphant but humble passage from simple house servant to Tom's savior is an outline for the heroic figure. He embodies all the qualities—loyalty, faith, love, compassion, strength, wisdom—of the dynamic hero, and his willingness to sacrifice his freedom and his life for two young boys establishes him as a classic benevolent character.

Both Huck and Jim can be viewed as the heroes of *Adventures of Huckleberry Finn*. But if the two characters are the chief agents of good, the loathsome Pap Finn is the novel's most pitiful and despicable character in terms of exemplifying the characteristics of a depraved, squalid world. When Pap reappears, with hair that is "long and tangled and greasy" and rags for clothes, it is a reminder of the poverty of Huck's initial existence and a realistic representation of the ignorance and cruelty that dominated the institution of slavery and prejudice in America. Pap is suspect of both religion and education and feels threatened by or resents Huck's ability to read and exist in the world of Miss Watson and the Widow Douglas.

Except for brief passages, however, readers are not privy to all of Pap's history and his rage at a world that he thinks has mistreated him. In a revealing sequence, Pap displays all of the con man's tactics when he tries to acquire Huck's reward money. Pap convinces a new judge that he is a changed man, has "started in on a new life," and has given his life to God. It only takes a night for Pap to return to his previous ways, as he becomes "drunk as a fiddler" and ends up collapsed outside the judge's house with a broken arm and a bitter spirit. The judge's observation that Pap might be reformed with the aid of a shotgun is a dark foreshadowing of what will follow.

Along with Pap's obvious insecurity toward Huck, what readers receive is a frightening picture of what Huck could become if left to the parental guidance of Pap. Huck's vague, past home life is solidified by Pap's constant verbal threats, and Pap warns Huck that he will physically abuse him if he tries to "put on considerble many frills." During the first meeting between the boy and his father, Pap's threats of abuse are so haphazard and disjointed that he becomes a comical figure. For Huck, the drunken rantings of Pap are neither astonishing nor cruel; they simply exist as a facet of his life, and Huck reports the threats with a tone of indifference and detachment.

Under the abusive eye of Pap, Huck attempts to romanticize a life free from the intrusions of a judgmental society and constrictive civilization. Away from the enforced rules of school and town, Huck is "free" to exist and absorb Pap's life of liquor and theft. But after Pap gets "too handy with his hick'ry," Huck decides to escape. The ensuing passages portray another comical, slapstick version of Pap, cursing against a "gov'ment" that would take his only son away and condemning a nation that would allow a "nigger" to vote. Beneath Pap's farcical ramblings, however, is the reality that Huck has, indeed, been constantly beaten and left alone for days, locked in the cabin. The reality of Huck's existence under Pap, then, is one where the presence of Pap's fist and racism pervade—where Huck is "all over welts" and subject to the venom Pap has for all of society.

Pap's role as an abusive parental figure is disturbing but vitally important to the novel, because it sets up as a direct contrast to the heroic and caring Jim. When Huck and Jim come upon the floating frame-house in Chapter 9, they discover a dead man among the various items. After Jim looks over the body, he tells Huck to come in the house, but "doan' look at his face—it's too gashly." Jim's gesture is similar to that of a protective parent, but the symbolism of the act is not fully realized until the last chapter of the novel. In Chapter the Last, Jim explains that the dead man aboard the house was Pap, and Huck realizes that Pap will not bother or abuse him ever again. With this realization, readers now view Jim's earlier gesture as an act performed by an empathetic and caring figure, and, in this sense, Jim serves as a father figure. With Jim as his role model, Huck is able to "inherit" the admirable and worthy qualities that Jim possesses and, therefore, is able to make his later decision to free Jim.

CliffsNotes Review

Use this CliffsNotes Review to test your understanding of the original text, and reinforce what you've learned in this book. After you work through the review and essay questions, identify the quote section, and the fun and useful practice projects, you're well on your way to understanding a comprehensive and meaningful interpretation of Adventures of Huckleberry Finn.

Q&A

1. At the beginning of the novel, why does Huck quit Tom Sawyer's gang?

   a. to paint a fence

   b. Pap forces him to quit

   c. Huck decides the gang is just pretend

2. Why does Huck think he'll go to hell if he helps Jim?

   a. Ssciety told him

   b. Jim told him

   c. the duke told him

3. What is ironic about the feud between the Grangerfords and Shepherdsons?

   a. the families are related

   b. the families are noble and educated

   c. the families own slaves

4. What role do the duke and the king play within the novel?

   a. they force Huck and Jim to continue down the river

   b. they give Huck and Jim money for steamship travel

   c. they protect Huck and Jim from con men

5. What does the raft/shore dichotomy symbolize?

   a. the peaceful raft and the squalid shore

   b. the number of times Huck and Jim board the raft

   c. the peaceful shore and the squalid raft

6. Why does Tom insist on an elaborate escape?

   a. so people will write realistic stories about them

   b. so Aunt Polly will be proud of him

   c. because that is the way it is done in romantic books

7. Why do the farmers not hang Jim at the end of the novel?

   a. because Jim has escaped up the Ohio River

   b. because Huck says he is a friend

   c. because Jim stayed with Tom when he shot

8. Why does Twain use the Mississippi River for the setting?

   a. because he knows the people and territory

   b. because it is the largest U.S. river

   c. because it was unchartered territory

Answers: (1) c. (2) a. (3) b. (4) a. (5) a. (6) c. (7) b. (8) a.

Identify the Quote

1. You don't know about me without you have read a book by the name of *The Adventures of Tom Sawyer*; but that ain't no matter.

2. The Widow Douglas, she took me for her son, and allowed she would sivilize me; but it was rough living in the house all the time, considering how dismal regular and decent the widow was in all her ways; and so when I couldn't stand it no longer, I lit out.

3. Sometimes the widow would take me one side and talk about Providence in a way to make a body's mouth water; but maybe next day Miss Watson would take hold and knock it all down again. I judged I could see that there was two Providences, and a poor chap would stand considerable show with the widow's Providence, but if Miss Watson's got him there warn't no help for him any more.

4. You're educated, too, they say; can read and write. You think you're better'n your father, now, don't you, because he can't? I'll take it out of you.

5. Dat truck dah is *trash;* en trash is what people is dat puts dirt on de head er dey fren's en makes 'em ashamed.

6. Next Sunday we all went to church, about three mile, everybody a-horseback. The men took their guns along, so did Buck, and kept them between their knees or stood them handy against the wall. The Shepherdsons done the same.

7. We said there warn't no home like a raft, after all. Other places do seem so cramped up and smothery, but a raft don't. You feel mighty free and easy and comfortable on a raft.

8. We say orgies now, in England. Orgies is better, because it means the thing you're after, more exact. It's a word that's made up out'n the Greek *orgo*, outside, open, abroad; and the Hebrew *jeesum*, to plant, cover up; hence in*ter*. So, you see, funeral orgies is an open er public funeral.

9. All right, then, I'll *go* to hell . . ..

10. They hain't no *right* to shut him up! *Shove!*—and don't you lose a minute. Turn him loose! he ain't no slave; he's as free as any cretur that walks this earth!

Answers: (1) [Huck, speaking to the reader and establishing himself as the first person narrator] (2)-[Huck, speaking to the reader, showing his distaste for society and civilization.] (3)-[Huck, speaking to the reader. This passage symbolizes the difference between compassionate and hypocritical religious teachings.] (4)-Pap, speaking to Huck. This quote symbolizes Pap's ignorance and insecurity toward education.] (5) [Jim, speaking to Huck, revealing his feelings of trust and friendship toward Huck and chastizing Huck for taking advantage of those feelings.] (6) [Huck, speaking to the audience, telling of the ironic feud of the Sherpherdsons and Grangerfords. The passage in particular symbolizes the hypocrisy of religion.] (7) [Huck, speaking to the reader, explaining the peacefulness and freedom aboard the raft.] (8) [the King, speaking to the people at Wilks' funeral, confusing the word "orgies" with "obsequies." This passage indicates the ignorance of the King and the townspeople who believe him.] (9) [Huck, to himself and the reader, as he reaches a decision about his responsibility toward Jim. This passage symbolizes Huck's gesture of sacrifice for Jim.] (10) [Tom, alerting the people around his bedstead, as well as the readers, that Jim has actually been freed by Miss Watson.]

Essay Questions

1. Compare and contrast the characters of Huckleberry Finn and Tom Sawyer.

2. Discuss the characteristics of Jim and how or if he qualifies as a heroic figure.

3. Discuss Huck's struggle with his conscience and how or if he qualifies as a heroic figure.

4. Compare and contrast the environment on shore and the environment on the raft.

5. Discuss Huck's statement, "All right, then, I'll *go* to hell."

6. Discuss the use of satire in the novel and how Twain uses different types of humor for social commentary.

7. Discuss the theme of romanticism versus realism.

8. Discuss Twain's use of Huck Finn as the narrator and how Huck's literal voice impacts the novel.

9. Discuss Huck's view of religion, especially his idea of two types of Providence and the characters that represent each type.

10. Discuss the novel as a realistic portrayal of American racism before *and* after the Civil War.

Practice Projects

1. Design your own Web site devoted to the study of *Adventures of Huckleberry Finn.* When considering what information to place on your site, think about the historical and contemporary issues of the novel. You should also consider the following questions: What links should you provide for your readers? How should your information be organized? What pictures, sketches, or maps should you make available? Would a time line of Mark Twain's life be helpful? Would a time line of slavery in the United States be helpful?

2. With the help of your classmates, find passages from the novel that detail the raft/shore dichotomy. It may be helpful to draw a map of the Mississippi River and use it to show when Huck and Jim are on the raft and when they are on shore. When considering what passages to use, examine Twain's differing descriptions of the river itself and of the river towns. You should also consider the following quesions: What sort of traits do the townspeople possess? What happens to Huck and Jim on the raft and the river? What happens to Huck and Jim on the shore? Are there exceptions and how are these important to the novel?

CliffsNotes Resource Center

The learning doesn't need to stop here. CliffsNotes Resource Center shows you the best of the best—links to the best information in print and online about the author and/or related works. And don't think that this is all we've prepared for you; we've put all kinds of pertinent information at www.cliffsnotes.com. Look for all the terrific resources at your favorite bookstore or local library and on the Internet. When you're online, make your first stop www.cliffsnotes.com where you'll find more incredibly useful information about *Adventures of Huckleberry Finn.*

Books

This CliffsNotes book, published by IDG Books Worldwide, Inc., provides a meaningful interpretation of *Adventures of Huckleberry Finn.* If you are looking for information about the author and/or related works, check out these other publications:

Mark Twain & Huck Finn, by Walter Blair. Although somewhat dated in terms of Twain's writing process, Blair's work is an important study of the novel's critical reception. The work also discusses the importance of Twain's childhood and his experiences with the Mississippi River. Berkeley and Los Angeles: University of California Press, 1960.

America's Humor: From Richard to Doonesbury, by Walter Blair and Hamlin Hill, examines the evolution of American Humor and is considered the most authoritative and important work for American Humor studies. Included in the study is a detailed chapter on Mark Twain and his literary predecessors. New York: Oxford University Press, 1978.

The Jim Dilemma: Reading Race in Huckleberry Finn, by Jocelyn Chadwick-Joshua, examines the issue of race and details the history of controversy surrounding *Adventures of Huckleberry Finn.* Jackson, MS: University Press of Mississippi, 1998.

The Critical Response to Mark Twain's Huckleberry Finn. Laurie Champion, ed. This is an expansive collection of critical studies of the novel from 1885 to 1991. Westport, Connecticut: Greenwood Press, 1991.

Mark Twain: The Fate of Humor, by James M. Cox, provides insight into Twain's method and outlook for humor in America. Princeton: Princeton University Press, 1966.

Writing Huck Finn: Mark Twain's Creative Process, by Victor A. Doyno, examines Twain's interrupted writing process in light of the 1991 discovery of the first half of the *Huck Finn* manuscript. Philadelphia: University of Pennsylvania Press, 1992.

Was Huck Black? Mark Twain and African-American Voices, by Shelley Fisher Fiskin, studies the African-American roots of the novel, including the controversial argument that the vernacular model for Huck was black. New York: Oxford University Press, 1993.

Mark Twain: God's Fool, by Hamlin Hill, examines in biographical detail the later years of Twain's life and career. This work also provides valuable insight into Twain's family tragedies and growing pessimism. New York: Harper and Row, 1975.

Huck Finn among the Critics: A Centennial Selection. M. Thomas Inge, ed. This book offers an annotated list of over 600 books and articles written about *Huck Finn.* Frederick, Maryland: University Publications of America, 1985.

Mr. Clemens and Mark Twain, by Justin Kaplan, is a Pulitizer-Prize winning biography that details the juxtaposition between the man, Sam Clemens, and the humorist, Mark Twain. New York: Simon and Schuster, 1966.

Satire or Evasion? Black Perspectives on Huckleberry Finn. James S. Leonard, Thomas A. Tenney, and Thadious M. Davis, eds. This is a collection of essays by leading African-American scholars. The essays address the controversy of *Huck Finn* in the classroom and historical and contemporary perspectives. Durham, NC: Duke University Press, 1992.

Coming to Grips with Huckleberry Finn: Essays on a Book, a Boy, and a Man, by Tom Quirk, examines the writing process, autobiographical influences, and the realism within the novel. The work concludes with a study of the political implications of teaching the novel. Columbia: University of Missouri Press, 1993.

One Hundred Years of Huckleberry Finn: The Boy, His Book, and American Culture. Robert Sattelmeyer and J. Donald Crowley, eds. Centennial publication includes several insightful essays on different aspects of the novel. Columbia: University of Missouri Press, 1985.

It's easy to find books published by IDG Books Worldwide, Inc.. You'll find them in your favorite bookstores (on the Internet and at a store near you). We also have three web sites that you can use to read about all the books we publish:

* www.cliffsnotes.com

* www.dummies.com

* www.idgbooks.com

Internet

Check out these Web resources for more information about Mark Twain and *Adventures of Huckleberry Finn*:

Mark Twain, http://marktwain.about.com—The most extensive site dedicated to the study of Mark Twain. Twain scholar, Jim Zwick, provides numerous links, including a history of banned books, historical contexts of the nineteenth century, Twain biographies and time lines, and the debate over *Huckleberry Finn* in the classroom. An excellent starting point for those interested in Mark Twain and his works.

Next time you're on the Internet, don't forget to drop by www.cliffs-notes.com. We created an online Resource Center that you can use today, tomorrow, and beyond.

Films and Plays

Huckleberry Finn, Paramount, 1920. A silent film with Lewis Sargent as Huck and George Reed as Jim.

Huckleberry Finn, Paramount, 1931. First sound production with Junior Durkin as Huck and Clarence Muse as Jim.

The Adventures of Huckleberry Finn, MGM, 1939. A film with Mickey Rooney as Huck and Rex Ingram as Jim.

The Adventures of Huckleberry Finn, MGM, 1960. First color production with Eddie Hodges as Huck and Archie Moore as Jim.

The Adventures of Huckleberry Finn, UA-Readers Digest, 1974. Jeff East as Huck and Paul Winfield as Jim.

Huckleberry Finn, ABC, 1975. TV adaptation with Ron Howard as Huck and Antonio Fargas as Jim.

Miller, Roger. *Big River.* 1984. A musical adaptation of the novel, which won a Tony award and is still performed in community theaters.

Adventures of Huckleberry Finn, PBS "American Playhouse," 1985. Miniseries with Patrick Day as Huck and Samm-Art Williams as Jim.

The Adventures of Huck Finn, Disney, 1993. Disney production with Elijah Wood as Huck and Courtney Vance as Jim.

Send Us Your Favorite Tips

In your quest for knowledge, have you ever experienced that sublime moment when you figure out a trick that saves time or trouble? Perhaps you realized you were taking ten steps to accomplish something that could have taken two. Or you found a little-known workaround that achieved great results. If you've discovered a useful tip that gave you insight into or helped you understand *Adventures of Huckleberry Finn* and you'd like to share it, the CliffsNotes staff would love to hear from you. Go to our Web site at www.cliffsnotes.com and click the Talk to Us button. If we select your tip, we may publish it as part of CliffsNotes Daily, our exciting, free e-mail newsletter. To find out more or to subscribe to a newsletter, go to www.cliffsnotes.com on the Web.

Index

G

H

I

J

L

M

CliffsNotes
@ cliffsnotes.com

CliffsNotes™

@ cliffsnotes.com

Check Out the All-New CliffsNotes Guides

TECHNOLOGY TOPICS

PERSONAL FINANCE TOPICS

CAREER TOPICS